A Germ of Goodness

LAW IN THE AMERICAN WEST

Series Editor

John R. Wunder,
University of Nebraska–Lincoln

Series Advisory Editors

Lawrence M. Friedman,
Stanford University
Kermit L. Hall,
University of Florida
Harry N. Scheiber,
University of California,
Berkeley

Volume 3

SHELLEY BOOKSPAN

A Germ of

Goodness

The California State Prison System, 1851–1944

University of Nebraska Press Lincoln & London

Library of Congress
Cataloging-in-Publication Data
Bookspan, Shelley, 1949–
A germ of goodness : the California state
prison system,
1851–1944 / Shelley Bookspan.
p.   cm. — (Law in the American West ; v. 3)
Includes bibliographical references (p.)
and index.
ISBN 0-8032-1216-X
1. Prisons—California—History—19th
century.
2. Prisons—California—History—20th
century.   I. Title.   II. Series.
HV9475.C2B66   1991
365'.9794—dc20   90-28876
                    CIP

CONTENTS

ILLUSTRATIONS

PREFACE

This book grew out of my desire to know more about the interaction between ideas and the physical world. My quest was not so much Cartesian as Mumfordian. I wanted to understand the relationships among attitudes, vision, planning, reality, and change, and prisons seemed to be places subject to all of these forces. Admittedly, when I began my study I felt some despair about the mutability of institutions, however dysfunctional, once they were monumentalized in granite or brick. My initial prejudice meant I would accept nothing less than that razing of the old prisons as evidence of change. Indeed, I still have no doubt that structure and infrastructure represent insidiously potent obstacles to achieving a grand, new world. Through the course of this work, though, I have had to learn to recognize when subtle changes are meaningful; I have had to learn to respect the slow and unsteady process of reevaluation that eventually underwrites reform. In studying change I have changed, and this has made the endeavor worthwhile for me.

Writing this book has been essentially a solitary task, but not a lonely one, thanks to the support and assistance of friends and colleagues. Rebecca Conard offered me welcome companionship during much of the research. Missy McDonald and Jamie Calhoun cheerfully and ably assisted me, especially with my newspaper research. Jamie also prepared the line drawings for the book. Patricia Cline Cohen and Karen Smith painstakingly read my early drafts and suggested many improvements, most of which I have had the sense to make. Robert Cashier and Ronald Nye, my associates at PHR Environmental, nobly endured my times of distraction. Paula Juelke Carr earned my special gratitude. In addition to preparing the index, Paula helped me find obscure biographical information, and she searched many a dusty haunt for photographs and illustrations. John R. Wunder, general editor of the Law in the American West series, invited me to submit my manuscript, and he recommended some crucial revisions (as well as publication).

Without doubt I also appreciate those who supported me less directly but with great regularity. My mother, Norma Schwartzberg, is proud of me. The quadrupeds in my life, Morpheus, Daisy, and Poppy, saw me through all stages of frustration and did their best to get me away from the computer when I needed a break. Mark Bookspan, my espoused, was, well, helpful, and it's not just because he brought me coffee.

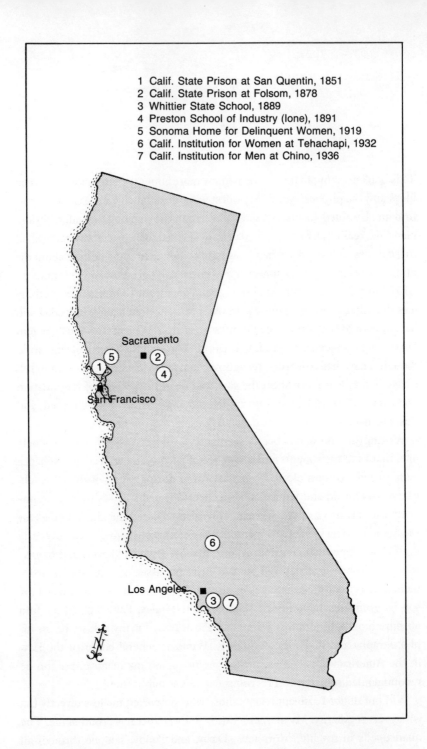

1 Calif. State Prison at San Quentin, 1851
2 Calif. State Prison at Folsom, 1878
3 Whittier State School, 1889
4 Preston School of Industry (Ione), 1891
5 Sonoma Home for Delinquent Women, 1919
6 Calif. Institution for Women at Tehachapi, 1932
7 Calif. Institution for Men at Chino, 1936

Sacramento

San Francisco

Los Angeles

Institutions of the California state prison system. (Map by Jamie Calhoun.)

To try to rear the changeling hope
In the cave of black despair
From Oscar Wilde, "The Ballad of Reading Gaol"

One of the central features of the United States is democracy, or government by the people, and one of the central features of the country's history is the expanding definition of "the people." Enfranchisement has evolved over the two-hundred-year history of the country to include more and different kinds of people. By way of constitutional amendments blacks, then women, and then youths over eighteen have gained the right to vote. Over time at the state level, ex-prisoners convicted of certain felonies have recovered their voting rights, and the vote is just one signal of the increasing inclusion of the criminally deviant into the mainstream of society. The thesis of this study is that the way in which the prisons themselves changed, in this case in California from the midnineteenth century to the midtwentieth century, also tells much about the evolution of American democracy. The story is full of twists, but it tells essentially of a change from the building of prisons as a form of exile to the building of prisons as corrective institutions designed to reintegrate the criminal into society.

For most of the ninety-three years between 1851, when the California State Legislature authorized "an act providing for securing the State Prison convicts," until 1944, when the legislature organized the state's four prisons into one adult penal system, the prisons at San Quentin and Folsom were the only places of incarceration for the state's felons.[1] The original concept for each of these institutions was as a stronghold, and, insofar as the legislature was willing to pay for them, they became imposing complexes of stone and brick. High masonry walls or guard towers unequivocally defined the institutions' boundaries, emulating the formidable stone exteriors of the nation's other prisons. The predominance of a plain, somber interpretation of the Gothic style for use as prison façades resulted from early prison designers' intention to reify the prisoners' experience, more than from an aesthetic sensibility. One eastern prison building committee ordained that "the exterior of a solitary prison should exhibit as much as possible great strength and convey to the mind a cheerless blank indicative of the misery which awaits the unhappy being who enters its walls."[2]

Early California legislators and much of the public adopted a view of criminals as a class unworthy of the blessings of liberty, one deserving such cheerlessness and needing to learn submission and obedience to authority. Accordingly, the prisons they built hearkened to an age of hierarchy and not democracy. Problems arose, however, as the American interpretation of democracy resounded increasingly of egalitarianism, and the seemingly impassable boundaries between good citizens and bad citizens began to erode. As that happened, gradually and not necessarily in linear fashion, stories of inhumanity within the prison walls motivated changes, and the notion of prisoner rehabilitation became less congruous with submissiveness and more so with developing the individual convict's ability to make informed, rational choices. California's struggle to develop an integrative kind of prison and prison system reflected the changing concept of a criminal from one who is inherently bad to one who is only, like everyone else, in part bad.

THE TWO NINETEENTH-CENTURY AMERICAN SYSTEMS

Deterrence and retribution were the hallmarks of colonial penal practice in America from the time the Puritans arrived from England. Physical punishment, like flogging or stockading, was painful and swift. Major crimes, such as theft, were as likely to be capital crimes as not. Such prisons as existed were, by intention, loathsome places. A premier example of a pre-Revolutionary prison was the Newgate colonial prison in Connecticut. Formed from abandoned copper mines in Simsbury, this prison crowded anywhere between thirty and one hundred inmates together in rock caverns seventy feet underground.

As one nineteenth-century observer of the Newgate facility noted: "The appearance of this place forcibly reminds the observer of the walls, castles and towers erected for the security of some haughty lordling of the feudal ages; while the gloomy dungeons within its walls call to remembrance a bastille or prison of the inquisition."[3]

The Revolution heralded reform of such conditions to some extent in all of the thirteen new states. Fittingly, this reform movement began in Pennsylvania, a legacy of colonial Founder William Penn's belief in the rehabilitation of criminals. Just after the Founding Fathers signed the Declaration of Independence, in 1776, the Pennsylvania Quakers initiated a state constitution calling for penal reform and thus began the planning for the first prison with an explicit program for rehabilitation as well as punishment. The Quakers intended for the Walnut Street Jail in Philadelphia to be a place where criminals, safely harbored from a vengeful society, would meditate on the *Holy Bible* and repent their wrongdoings. It would be, in other words, a penitentiary.

In order to enhance this opportunity for prisoners to purge their souls and to preclude their communion with other felons, the Quakers developed what came to be known as the Pennsylvania, or solitary, system. The Walnut Street Jail, which opened in 1791, contained sixteen cells, each measuring six feet by eight feet by nine feet. Each was to hold a single penitent, although jail population statistics suggest that either frequent turnover or doubling occurred. Each prisoner was to work at some assigned task, also in solitude, in separate daytime cells and benefit from regular visits from brethren and ministerial guards.

During the same time period, Thomas Jefferson and Benjamin Latrobe, both architects and champions of liberalism, discussed an alternative prison style. Latrobe designed the State Penitentiary at Richmond, Virginia, in 1797–98. Although his design provided for three tiers of small, individual cells arranged in a semicircle for maximum visibility, he did also consider human contact essential and provided some dormitory rooms for the more reformed prisoners. The prison's exterior was nonetheless ponderous: "To form the entrance gate, an enormous stone arch without molded embellishment of any kind sprang from the foundation line in a bold lateral sweep. The effect was of awesome strength."[4]

Neither Jefferson nor Latrobe promulgated an alternative prison program to accompany this design, however, and subsequent architects accepted the Quakers' concept of solitude instead. When the British-born architect John Haviland designed Pennsylvania's Eastern Penitentiary, authorized in 1821, in a manner "to perpetuate the best traditions of medieval castle architecture," he offered a large-scale architectural integration of the Gothic exterior with an interior accommodating the solitary system. His hub-and-spoke, or radial, plan provided for well-separated individual cells along the spokes, themselves conducive to keen surveillance by guards stationed at the hub.

The cells, although intended for solitary habitation, were much more generous than those of the Walnut Street Jail. They measured eight feet by twelve
feet by ten feet and contained primitive water closets. Unlike Walnut Street,
however, where prisoners worked daily outside their little cells, prisoners in
the Eastern Penitentiary were not to leave their accommodations throughout
their stay.[5]

Generally this radial design and solitary program received more attention
and emulation in Europe than it did in America; repentance and, especially,
enforced idleness, did not suit American penal objectives, which included
prison self-sufficiency through profitable and in-house use of prison labor.
In addition, buildings such as Haviland's and Latrobe's were expensive, designed as they were to serve the needs of the individual penitent. Americans often resented spending money to provide for what they considered the
comfort of those who had forfeited their individual rights. The Pennsylvania
system did not successfully reform prisoners as the Quakers had planned,
anyway, in part because of internal corruption. At least by 1844, with the
founding of the New York Prison Association, many of the new generation of
Quakers had repudiated the concept.[6]

In spite of the problems with the Pennsylvania system, American legislators generally embraced the concept of solitary incarceration. By 1818, the
state of New York had developed a rival interior architectural scheme for its
prison at Auburn that, when combined with "the rule of silence," became the
model for prisons across the country. In response to an entrepreneur who
proposed to run a factory inside the prison, Auburn's warden, Elam Lynds,
and his deputy, John Cray, invented the silent system, which informed the
1825 design of Sing Sing. Within cell blocks the Auburn system imposed
solitary confinement; without, Auburn accommodated congregate dining and
congregate labor, but imposed an intimidating regimen of silence in order to
preclude rapport among prisoners and to promote meditation.

The simpler architecture required for the Auburn system as well as the
work ethic it sustained appealed to American legislators. Soon prisons across
the country borrowed the architectural and penal scheme developed in New
York, and it handily supplanted the Pennsylvania system. It was the Auburn
ideal that motivated the theories of California prison policymakers throughout the nineteenth century.[7]

THE HISTORIOGRAPHY OF THE ORIGINS OF PRISONS

The post-Revolutionary origins and development of the penitentiary system have intrigued a number of recent historians whose work addresses the operational relationship between incarceration and democracy. In his important scholarship, David J. Rothman has presented the powerful thesis that Jacksonian-era reformers embraced the penitentiary, among other asylums, as a way to interject order into the larger society during a time of rapid change.[8] The very chaos of the lives of social deviants, according to the reformers, threatened everyone's stability, and everyone would benefit by their exposure to an ordered life in a protected environment. This thesis accords well with the origination of American prisons and implies a widespread timidity about the democratic ideals of the Revolution. Where a deviant population was heterogeneous, the white community tended to see deviance not so much as the effect of chaos, but as the cause. Deviance and foreign customs often were indistinguishable; prisons and other asylums, Rothman argued, served as places of unity and regimentation.

The French scholar Michel Foucault also presented a sophisticated social control thesis, but he viewed penitentiaries more as insidious devices by which to induce self-discipline in the larger population than as institutions in which a few would learn orderly behavior.[9] "The luminaries who invented liberty also invented discipline," he asserted. Liberty would only work in a population capable of self-control, otherwise anarchy would prevail. Those who internalized society's rules became the middle classes. Of course, society's rules reflected middle class social norms in turn, and thus a system developed in which misfits served as foils for the obedient middle class who themselves were agents of the luminaries. Prisons encaging those misfits represented an oppressive society of external controls and menaced anyone with wavering self-control.

Dario Melossi and Massimo Pavarini also employed a class analysis, but in a more traditionally Marxian way.[10] Noting the concomitant rise of penitentiaries and the industrial economy and the need in both to observe a strict regimen, they argued that prison sentencing can only occur in a society that can evaluate a person's time; with the rise of the factory, time became a measure of industrial productivity, and thus something with an inherent value. Prisons, they argued, were mock factories—some, like Auburn, were even real factories—in which inmates learned the habits of industry and thus the value of their time. In nineteenth-century America this was very much a moral lesson. Individual penitents learned the price of their prodigality. Similarly, John A. Conley has argued that the growth, development, shape, and functions of nineteenth-century prisons mirrored the industrialization of society.[11]

The notion that prisons reflect a predominant social morphology in an explicit way is an insight Michael Stephen Hindus also offered in a recent study. Hindus theorized that instead of mock factories, prisons were mock plantations, that is, mock slave societies.[12] In South Carolina, slavery during the Revolutionary and Jacksonian eras obviated the need for prisons such as those Massachusetts built. Slavery served the function in South Carolina of delineating the power structure within that society. Massachusetts had the same requirement, but it had no analogous ranking system. The prison, however, identified and isolated a class of subservient people, removed from them their freedom and privileges of citizenship, and thereby helped stabilize an existing, unegalitarian political order.

Whether the analysis has been predominantly social, intellectual, economic, or political, historians have tended to understand prisons as microcosms of some ideal hierarchy. These analyses very usefully connect the opposing allures of freedom and the safety of authority. Most of these analyses, however, derive from the prison histories of eastern states, where a sense of community preceded rapid growth, change, and apparent chaos. When the village idiot was a cousin, he would be kept, if not out of love, then out of duty. But when he was unknown and, perhaps, spoke a strange tongue as well, he was feared. Where new criminal codes sprung from this basic emotion of fear, such as in California, it was arguably the happenstance of democracy that initially made incarceration, rather than execution or maiming, the prescribed punishment for the criminally deviant.

PRISONS IN THE WEST

The penology of the eastern states reflected the old tradition of community responsibility in addition to the newer value of individualism. In the western territories, the succession of values was reversed. White male adventurers uncommitted to most social values other than fortune-seeking opened passages throughout the West. Other such individuals followed suit, and boom towns arose where economic opportunity seemed most promising. While the history of the settlement of the West is full of sectarian community building, it is also fundamentally characterized by these rugged individuals, many of whom were misfits from the East. Eastern penology, designed to reinforce conformity, did not necessarily translate well in the West, but it was the only penology readily available.

The federal government was in great part responsible for bringing eastern penology west. It supplied plans for such western territorial prisons as Colorado's at Canon City, authorized in 1868 and Wyoming's at Rawlins, authorized in 1888. These prisons, at least in their construction, thus reflected the Auburn system of solitary cells, congregate dining and labor, and silence. Where the states themselves gave consideration to prison planning, they also looked east. The state of Kansas, which opened its penitentiary in 1883, had sent officials to examine eastern prison plans and eventually copied the new Joliet, Illinois, version of the Auburn system.

With the one-man-per-cell system, prisons in the burgeoning West rapidly grew overcrowded. Characteristic of the West, too, legislators proved generally uninterested in expanding prison facilities to maintain the one-man-per-cell Auburn ideal. In California, only white prisoners received the benefit of the one-man-per-cell ideal; foreign-born or black prisoners suffered with several cellmates in tiny rooms designed for one.

In several western prisons, in fact, there was ongoing experimentation with methods to avoid paying for operations as well as facilities. These experiments tended to be controversial for nonpenological reasons. Missouri, for example, for a period of four years beginning in 1839, leased its prison and prisoners to a pair of entrepreneurs who profited by selling cheap prison labor. Work off-premises made escape opportune, and the system broke down for lack of control. In several other states, Colorado being a prime example, the ethic that demanded that prisoners work and sustain themselves (perhaps even turn a profit for the state) confronted the equal demand that prison labor not compete with free labor. The result, after considerable conflict among legislators, prison administrators, and the public, was the identification of certain select work tasks or products that free labor agreed to relinquish, such as road building under dangerous conditions.

In all, the potential for rehabilitation, which had been central to the general acceptance of the Auburn system in the East (but which was poorly realized everywhere), was of less importance in the West, where the individual convict was not necessarily expected to become integrated into the larger community.[13]

THE CALIFORNIA STATE PRISON SYSTEM

In general, California experienced the clash between eastern cultural values, rugged individualism, and foreign influences to a greater extent than any other western state or territory. California enjoyed a reputation as a land of health, beauty, and opportunity even before the gold rush of 1849 heralded unprecedented population growth. The origins of the California state prison system indicate that its creators' need to control a deviant population was primary, and the subsequent history shows how rehabilitation developed gradually as a goal.

In 1852, California's prison inspectors submitted their first annual report, and in it they made explicit the need for prisons to separate the alien and the deviant from the rest of society. In a lengthy aside, they recommended that California enact laws to prohibit "importation into this state of foreign convicts, or of those other persons belonging to alien and servile races" in order to avoid crimes against a state whose laws "patent their inferiority." The inspectors contended that "the degraded races have always needed the jailer and executioner, and been conspicuous for improvidence and crime." [14] Their solution was to bar "the free negroes of the United States and the peons of neighboring republics" rather than change the laws that such people, they predicted, would inevitably violate.

California, of course, was unable to prevent the immigration of alien and deviant people, and, at first, the California State Prison at San Quentin was little more than a depository for the hated and unwanted. Prison statistics in 1858 showed that only 45 percent of San Quentin's prisoners were born in the United States. By 1873 that percentage had increased, but only to 53 percent. The realization of the Auburn system in such a heterogeneous state represented a reform goal prized into the twentieth century, long after eastern penologists themselves rejected the system. As long as the sense of criminals as unassimilable aliens prevailed it was self-fulfilling. There could be no popular acceptance of the penitentiary goal of rehabilitation. The prison only incidentally served even retributive goals because such aliens were not seen as treasuring the liberty of which incarceration deprived them.

Once in place, the custodial prisons at San Quentin and Folsom seemed essential to the protection of society, and they remain maximum security institutions today. The major reform that occurred in the first one-hundred years of the California prison system was the development of institutions and flexible laws to distinguish among individual prisoners and to provide to some extent for their distinctive needs. To surpass mere custodial goals required a greater tolerance of deviance within the native population and a greater willingness, born of experience, to assimilate the alien.

Before there was serious challenge to the custodial system in California, the Auburn system was obsolete. In the East, the system had endured two generations of prison reformers, the penologists of the Golden Age and those of the Progressive Era. These two generations molded together a penological program based on a blend of environmental determinism and individual responsibility. The program included graded prisons and nonprison options, such as probation and parole, that together laid the theoretical groundwork for building two minimum security prisons in California in the 1930s. The women's prison at Tehachapi and the men's prison at Chino had no cell blocks and no prison walls, but rather dormitories and fences. These facilities, so different from San Quentin and Folsom, betokened a liberalizing society, and the subsequent establishment of a centralized prison authority demonstrated the state's willingness to create an integrated prison system.

This is the story of the fits, starts, penury, and personality struggles through which California developed a prison system to assess and address individual needs while retaining its custodial institutions. It is a story of the West, even though eastern penology, with all of its overtones of moral duty, provided the language for prison reform. In a state where chaos preceded the assertion of normative rule, fear, not hope, formed the governing principal of penology. It is a story of America because true reform rested on an expanded sense of individual potential. As one nineteenth-century San Quentin warden observed, "Every man has within him a germ of goodness," and thus nineteenth-century California possessed the germ of prison reform.[15]

1

The Building of San Quentin, 1850–1872

All that we know who lie in jail
Is that the wall is strong
From Oscar Wilde, "The Ballad of Reading Gaol"

Initial prison-building occurred in the new state of California without much attention to penological theory. Many of the state's early politicians had come from the East, like the gold seekers, to exploit economic opportunity. Many had been exposed, at least in passing, to penitentiary-type prisons, but such prisons reflected a more ordered, less ambiguous set of social circumstances. In San Francisco, where most of the Argonauts docked, the population rose from about two thousand in February 1849 to perhaps as many as thirty thousand by the end of the year. A large percentage of these immigrants were transient men, seeking fortune and good times. In this atmosphere, as woolly as the wild West got, criminal justice was often as lawless as any criminal activity.

The infamous hundred-day reign of San Francisco's Committee of Vigilance in 1851 represented the frustration and fear of citizens faced with the threat of immigrants, uncontrolled crime, and an ineffectual government. "Sydney ducks," former Australian criminals seeking fortune and promising menace in California, were particularly the objects of the Committee's extralegal vengeance. The committee itself originally consisted of about one hundred men, usually characterized as ordinary, intelligent citizens, and its ranks swelled as others rallied to the idea of quick elimination of the foreign rogues. After the election of 1852, legally elected authorities adopted the committee's goals of law enforcement and thus supplanted the vigilantes.[1] One outgrowth of official attention to law enforcement was the San Francisco County Jail. Another was the State Prison.

In 1851 California's state constitution was only two years old, and official statehood was but months old. Even so, as the country's El Dorado, California was growing incrementally. Fortune seekers did not necessarily make the best citizens, as San Franciscans concluded quickly about the Australians. In that year the state legislature heard it reported that "California . . . is infested by hordes of the most desperate scoundrels accomplished in every act of villainy." Undoubtedly there was some truth to the contention that "convicts from the penal colonies and outlaws from all parts of the world have emigrated in numbers to this country, attracted by the fable of our riches and lust for plunder."[2]

Governor John McDougal, who had served as superintendent of the modified Auburn-style Indiana State Prison in the 1840s, infuriated the members of the Committee of Vigilance when he refused to support their extralegal activities. McDougal insisted that the new state needed a prison immediately in which to isolate the villains from society. Legislators agreed and, on April 25, 1851, passed "An Act providing for securing the State Prison Convicts" to accompany a newly promulgated penal code.[3]

The young state's coffers barely jingled, however, and construction and maintenance of a prison promised to be no insignificant expense. Other rapidly settled frontier states had developed a system of leasing their convicts to a private contractor who would provide for their security and care in return for the use of their labor.[4] On McDougal's suggestion, the California legislature followed this lead and accepted the offer of a one hundred thousand-dollar bond from two politically active former Mexican war heroes, Mariano Guadalupe Vallejo and James Madison Estell. These men saw an entrepreneurial opportunity in exploiting prison labor, and on the state's acceptance of the bond, they became prisoners' lessees.

Under the specific conditions of the lease, Estell and Vallejo received promise of a state-constructed prison and unrestricted use of convict labor. They would, in turn, quarter and feed the state's prisoners; submit to regular inspection by the Board of Inspectors of the State Prison, three paid delegates selected by the Governor; and report annually to the legislature.

This deal seemed potentially lucrative to the lessees and advantageous to the state as well. In 1852, however, when he saw that his namesake town would not become the state capital, Vallejo withdrew entirely from public affairs. Subsequently, Estell and several others, including now-former Governor McDougal, purchased Vallejo's interest in the prisoners.

Estell retained controlling interest in the lease. He soon formed the San Francisco Manufacturing Company to capitalize on convict labor and commenced accepting prisoners from the six county jails throughout the state, even before the selection of a prison site. There ensued from this arrangement with Estell an administrative and legal struggle lasting for a decade. In the young state, government itself was new and even occasionally lawless, as the Committee of Vigilance had been. The chaos and the legal wranglings of the 1850s in regard to San Quentin reflected official floundering. The focus of penological concerns on the custodial end reflected a broader need for public officials to gain control of public affairs.[5]

CALIFORNIA PLANS A PRISON

During the 1851 legislative session, an act had passed "to secure the state prisoners." Early in the 1852 session, legislators passed an act "to provide for the erection of a State Prison."[6] That law authorized the establishment of the Board of Prison Commissioners, who had the authority to choose a site of not more than twenty acres, to prepare suitable building plans, and to advertise for and select a building contractor. While the commission was making its decisions, however, deputies from the jails in San Francisco, San Jose, Monterey, Santa Barbara, Los Angeles, and San Diego, paid by the mile for their escort services, brought an abundance of prisoners to Estell and his sublessees, Colonel John Hays and Major John Caperton. The sublessees in turn placed the prisoners aboard a ship, the Waban. The ship had a capacity of perhaps fifty, but soon more than three times that many convicts languished there. According to a popular account, the prisonkeepers discovered the point at San Quentin accidentally.[7] The ship, moored in the Sacramento River, was so burdened with bodies that it drifted uncontrollably until landing at Quentin Point, across the bay from San Francisco, whereupon the overseers discovered brick clay and declared the site acceptable for a permanent prison. Other, more reliable accounts indicate that the location provided easy access to an existing quarry on Angel Island, and a tug pulled the ship across the San Francisco Bay to be harbored there.[8]

Without much controversy, the San Quentin site became the official prison site in 1852. A letter dated June 20, 1852, from Horace W. Carpentier, an attorney and the first mayor of Oakland, who chaired the commission, to the new governor, John Bigler, makes clear that the official party inspected and chose the site among other candidate locations. Carpentier's two associate commissioners, James S. Graham and former governor McDougal's brother George, selected the ten-acre San Quentin parcel while Carpentier, who had been unable to visit there himself, favored a location on Bull's Head point, near Martinez in Contra Costa County. The Bull's Head site consisted of twenty acres and an "abundance of lime and building stone." N. B. Smith, Esq., had offered to donate the land to the state expressly for the purpose of building a prison there. Nonetheless, apparently having reason to fear a title dispute over the Bull's Head property, Governor Bigler ordered the purchase of the San Quentin site.[9]

James Graham, who was also the superintendent of public buildings, had had the responsibility for procuring a design for the permanent prison. After the selection of the site he hired architect Reuben Clark to draw plans for a complete state prison complex. Clark was an easterner who had worked with the renowned and prolific neoclassicist Charles Bulfinch, and had arrived in California with the crowds in 1849. Bulfinch had designed a state prison for Massachusetts, built in Charlestown in 1805. His plan provided small dormitory rooms, encouraging some camaraderie among the inmates. The Massachusetts Building Commissioners, however, abandoned the Bulfinch plan in favor of Auburn when adding the north wing.[10]

Clark's apprenticeship had thus exposed him to more than one of the eastern ways to build prisons. Nothing in the Clark plan, however, suggests any hospital, chapel, or workshop facilities, so his was not an attempt to develop a self-contained prison system. Instead, it seems that Clark designed a secure complex to accommodate in solitude the existing number of prisoners and to separate the men from the women as provided for by the 1852 act. His plans called for a prison wall with four watchtowers, one atop each corner, which he subsequently told a legislative committee in 1853 he estimated would cost $210,775; a keeper's house with a watchtower atop it, to cost $47,275; a male prisoners' building with 140 iron doors and 280 locks, to cost $272,717; a female prisoners' building with 9 iron doors and 18 locks, to cost $19,345; an unspecified number of privies, to cost $1,152; and miscellaneous other fees totaling $18,736. Clark's total estimate, then, for completion of his plan was over $570,000.[11]

Graham approved Clark's plan, even though Carpentier, the chair of the commission, believed the specifications were "upon too magnificent a scale." Moreover, Carpentier was of the opinion that the legislature, in authorizing the 1852 act, had actually voted for a one hundred thousand-dollar spending limit that had not appeared in the published version of the law. It was clear to Carpentier, even before seeing Clark's estimates, that the realization of the entire Clark plan would far exceed that amount. When Graham proceeded to advertise for contractors' bids anyway, there followed the first of many scandals associated with the first decade of the State Prison.[12]

Initially the winning contractor, Ferdinand Vassault, a man with whom lessee Estell had some financial ties, had bid more than $1,000,000 to complete the project. While his was the highest bid among a handful, the lower bidders withdrew their offers, presumably having received some compensation in return. After a rancorous debate, with Carpentier angrily refusing to agree to such a price, the commission decided to readvertise the project. Vassault lowered his bid to $725,000 and submitted it against only one competitor, whom the commissioners disqualified for an unspecified reason. Still Carpentier balked at the high price and wrote a letter alerting Governor Bigler that he felt obliged under the law to authorize an outrageous contract with Vassault since, by advertising, the commission had committed the state to Clark's plan. Carpentier begged Bigler to intervene and allow Vassault to complete at most a minimum of the proposed structures.[13]

Vassault had cleared the land in preparation for construction when, during the 1853 legislative session, the contract amount came to light. The executive branch ordered Vassault to stop work while a select committee of the senate examined the prison grounds and while the senate heard testimony about whether the 1852 act indeed should have contained language specifying a one hundred thousand-dollar spending limit for construction of the prison. Most of the solons interviewed remembered that such a limit had indeed passed, and the suspicion was great that somehow bribery accounted for the omission of the limit from the final published law. As a consequence, Vassault lost his contract, the original commissioners lost their positions, and the state lost whatever commitment it had had to the Clark plan.[14]

CALIFORNIA BUILDS A PRISON

The 1853 Report of the Select Committee to Examine the State Prison announced that the inspectors had reviewed the San Quentin site and found the Marin County location "in every respect suitable for such a purpose." Although the absence of water power and isolation from agricultural or industrial society were to burden the lessee and his sublessees with idle convicts, the legislature's 1853 committee also noted with approval that "the place is somewhat secluded and will be easily guarded."[15]

This criterion, "easily guarded," became the one most valued when nineteenth-century Californians located, evaluated, and reformed their prisons, if not when they constructed them. That same 1853 Select Committee report evinced some sentiment for the 157 prisoners crammed unhealthily into the hull of a prison ship, saying that "humanity alone should cause the State to push forward the [building of a permanent prison]." Nonetheless, the report revealed the committee members' belief that almost by definition the convicts' humanity was itself so tenuous as to require constant vigilance. Although (according to 1855 statistics) prisoners convicted of murder, mayhem, manslaughter, or other violent crimes represented only 17 percent of the inmate population, the committee's concerns reflected the opinion that the convicts were a vicious lot. "Should these men overpower their guard," the committee worried, "they would spread devastation throughout the County in which they are located." The first few years of leasehold administration served only to exacerbate these fears.[16]

This particular committee, although it opined that prisoners were a vicious, dangerous lot and offered "easily guarded" as the initiating principle of California prison building, it also proposed creating a system of prison labor "not only to render the prison self-supporting but reformatory."[17] Before California's first prison building stood ready for habitation, California's legislators had thus enunciated a fundamental conflict of goals that would persist for the next one hundred years: punishment versus reformation. The former goal required no special theories or expertise, just a stronghold. The latter goal, however, required the facilities and furnishings for teaching prisoners how to cope with a paradoxical moral imperative: submitting to authority while assuming personal responsibility in a free society.

Soon Golden Age reform penologists in the East began to transform their ideas about the kinds of prisons that could reconcile both ends, and some

California solons and reformers were to follow suit. The view of the 1853 committee, however, typically did not make note of any inconsistency. Rather, the committee failed to recommend funding for any vocational training programs, and in its penury the legislature refused to effect its own penological prescriptions.[18]

Ironically, legislative penury also undermined the committee's foremost goal of building a stronghold. In an unrealistic or, perhaps, disingenuous way, the legislature persisted in planning for a prison population of fifty, even while the prison ship and temporary quarters housed three times that many convicts. As a consequence, the lawmakers failed to allocate funds adequate to build secure facilities to accommodate the existing prison population, even while tacitly endorsing plans for a larger, more fortified facility.

In principle, the 1853 legislative committee had generally endorsed the Clark plan, but suggested that the contractor eliminate detail work as a money-saving device: "As regards the [prison] plan in its general details, it is good; but a very large sum of money may be saved by confining the work to a plain substantial building," the committee reported, while suggesting the elimination of "all such superfluities as Roman towers on the corners," which the designer had considered safety features as well as important architectural statements.[19]

In fact, after the scandal over the Vassault contract, the wary legislature only authorized funding to complete one main cell building. This building's specifications described a brick rectangle containing two rows of twenty-four cells on the second floor and an undifferentiated first floor, measuring 170 by 28 feet. This first cell block quickly gained the nickname, "the Stones." The Stones opened in 1854 and remained in use until 1959. Each cell was on the second floor and measured nearly 6 by 9 feet, or about 54 square feet, a size suggesting solitary occupancy since solitary eastern cells typically measured from 7 by 7 feet to 7 by 10 feet, or from 49 to 70 square feet. With the first floor open and adaptable for congregate labor and dining, the plan suggests an intention to effect the Auburn system at San Quentin, but without the security of a cell house enclosing the cell block or watch towers on the future walls. The absence of a cell house was an architectural compromise originated in Baltimore to ameliorate the costs of prison building and employed in some of the more temperate states, such as Georgia.[20]

If, as Estell, the lessee and now the warden, noted in his 1855 report to the legislature, "it was not contemplated that there would be to exceed fifty prisoners, at any one time, for years," then each cell was indeed intended for solitary habitation. The legislators may have imagined that their original hopeful prediction of 50 prisoners at a time could be achieved, even when more than 150 occupied temporary quarters. Certainly, throughout the decade, even as the prisoner population grew, the state returned to its estimate of 50 prisoners when dealing with public outcry about San Quentin. This prediction proved increasingly difficult to defend as experience proved it wrong. Whether it was because of the mileage allowance, or the eagerness of localities to be rid of undesirable newcomers, or the impressive roster of possible state crimes, the lessee soon found himself inundated with prisoners to house, clothe, and feed.[21]

Estell was appalled at the abundance of prisoners and at the belief of many citizens and legislators alike that he was obliged to construct prison accommodations for them all. Although Estell had agreed in this first contract to erect "suitable temporary buildings upon the grounds herewith leased, or shall have suitable and secure Prison ships or vessels," the state had assumed the responsibility for building the permanent prison. Perhaps it was simply because state officials did not want to spend three-quarters of a million dollars on building adequate prison facilities that they continued to predict a need to house only fifty convicts. In any case, the Stones was inadequate to hold the prison population at one to a cell.[22]

THE CONTRACT SYSTEM FAILS

The 1851 law establishing the state prison required that the prison lessee feed, clothe, and maintain securely the state prisoners until such time as the state should erect a prison building. It also explicitly granted the lessee the right to sell convict labor outside the prison grounds without specifying that that right should end upon the erection of a prison. According to the seventh section, the act was not to be "so construed as to confine the labor of the prisoners within the limits of said prison, or to any particular place or labor." This meant, as an 1855 committee of prison inspectors observed, that the lessee believed he could work his convicts as file clerks in San Francisco rather than as laborers in the brick yard at San Quentin if he so chose. Estell had in fact made liberal use of his own version of the Irish "trusty" system in which "a prisoner, whose term of service is about expiring, or who has behaved well, or has been recommended to the lessee as a gentleman and a man of good standing and family, is permitted to do light work, to be kept separate from the mass of prisoners, to go on errands for miles in the country, on foot or on horseback, alone; to go to San Francisco, to sleep without the guard at the cook house, off the Prison grounds." [23]

By 1855, the state finally agreed that the only way legally to put an end to the capricious use and keeping of the state's prisoners was to buy Estell's contract from him and assume control of the prison. All involved or interested parties seemed to concur in the necessity of such a move. Marin County residents had fiercely denounced Estell and the prison during grand jury proceedings early that year. Governor Bigler recommended termination of the lease. He appointed a Special Committee to investigate and report on options for the prison. That committee and the standing Board of State Prison Inspectors both encouraged a new, state-controlled endeavor. What's more, Estell himself longed for relief from his contract responsibilities.

Everyone seemed to believe that the prison and prisoners were out of control and to fear the consequences of escapes and uprisings. When Estell submitted his annual report that year, he claimed that the prison population exceeded three hundred. In order to house this abundance of prisoners Estell had anchored the prison ship off Marin Island, keeping, among others, the handful of woman prisoners there. Otherwise, he made the following use of the Stones: "This wing contains forty-eight cells, capable of containing four prisoners each. There is one large room below, capable of holding one hundred, but without a division." [24] Such crowding only served to elevate the criterion "easily guarded" to an ideal shared by Estell and much of the free society.

As Estell made very clear in his report, mass escape and mayhem had become for him an ominous spectre. Of the first floor holding, without division, one hundred prisoners, he wrote, "This room, of course, if broken would allow the whole number to escape. Thus situated, we are in the most imminent danger." In fact, the prospect of escape dominated Estell's report. Ninety-eight prisoners had escaped, he asserted, since 1851; forty-one were unsuccessful, and "quite a number . . . killed in attempts to suppress revolts, and in efforts to retake those who had escaped." While he did not offer a tally of the number killed, the state's prison inspectors, in their 1855 report, suggested that they believed many more had been killed than Estell was willing to report.[25]

Estell's fear of escape was so profound that he avoided making the most profitable use of prison labor. During periods of heavy fog, for example, he refused to allow prisoners out of their cells, even keeping them from taking their meals at nearby mess tents. He even reported, unabashedly, of one full week during which he had deprived prisoners of their meals, lest they escape in the fog. They would probably have not got very far after a week without food. Nonetheless, Estell made no apologies, but instead recommended building fortified prisons as the only way to insure against the danger of escape. "Instances are known of prisoners, condemned for life, having served out the term of their existence without any attempt to regain their liberty," Estell marvelled, "but it is always in prisons, built in the strongest manner and guarded with eternal vigilance."[26]

Crowded conditions, fear of rebellion, and isolation from the marketplace made it impossible for Estell to employ his convicts very profitably. As a result of his disappointment in the profitability of the prison and because of new legislative attempts to constrain the prison operations, Estell offered to return his contract to the state for a sum of $127,000, payable in 7 percent bonds. This was an offer the Special Committee of 1855 decided to consider.

In hearings before the two committees investigating the state prison issue, witness after witness testified to the system's evils. The comparative freedom that some San Quentin inmates seemed to enjoy offended the California legislators and many citizens who expected prisoners to be continually incarcerated, and thereby punished and out of harm's way.[27] Unless convicted felons were assured of detention within a prescribed place of punishment then the established system violated the fundamental principle of prison building: the safe-keeping of the convicts.

Certainly the free citizens of Marin County agreed that the prison needed to be explicitly separate from their society. In light of the many prison escapes and frequent reports in the *San Francisco Bulletin* about Estell's questionable behavior and management, the county had appointed a grand jury to investigate the San Quentin prison and its effect on the local citizens. The official prison committees heard the admonishments of the grand jury for the state to "take charge of her own institution" or at least to compel the lessee "to build, immediately, good and substantial walls around said prison, and safe and secure cells for said convicts."

Noting, moreover, that county residents had never consented to the prison location, that the government had promised that the maximum prisoner population would be fifty, and that the citizens of Marin County lived in "hourly dread of their lives and property, and their wives and families from assault and violation," the indignant grand jury sounded an early warning about citizen rebellion and further resounded intolerance of competition between free and convict labor.[28]

Estell's San Francisco Manufacturing Company, begun on the promise of bidding for contracts using convict labor, seemed a shocking venture to the Marin citizens. They could not believe "it was ever the object and intention of the Legislature . . . to bring the labor of a class of desperadoes and villains who have been consigned by the laws of the land . . . to infamy and disgrace, in conflict with the labor and interest of the poor laboring, but respectable and law-abiding class of the community." It was of little concern to them that the San Francisco Manufacturing Company was in grave financial trouble because of Estell's inability to control the many convicts he found himself forced to secure.[29]

Additional testimony before the 1855 committee came from guards and former guards of the State Prison. The committee heard about the sexual relations between one or two of the guards and one or two of the female convicts (by then free), about the frequent intoxication of some guards and even some prisoners, about Estell's operation of a for-profit prison bar, about the suspected embezzlement and bribe-taking among prison officers, and, most certainly, about the capriciousness of Estell's discipline. Estell's misuse of the trusty system meant some favored prisoners served as their own guards; many witnesses attributed the numerous escapes to the impossibility of overseeing a trusty system in a wall-less prison employing few nonconvict guards. In one instance, a former prison superintendent claimed, "I received instructions, both verbal and written, relative to the treatment of convicts. Gardner [for example] was put in for manslaughter July 1854; General Estell wrote me that Gardner was a gentleman, and I must not put him in a cell."[30]

An affair particularly notorious for revealing the lack of systematic discipline within the prison was that of Thomas McFarland Foley, a young man convicted of killing a San Francisco newspaper editor. Estell treated Foley with especial favor, apparently at the behest of a local judge. First, Estell ordered that Foley "have all the liberties" of the place and that it not be generally known he was a prisoner. As Foley himself told Judge Elcan Heydenfeldt, his benefactor, "[Estell] gave orders that I should live at his hotel, outside the guards, and receive the same fare, after the officers, in the dining room. . . . Now, all that is necessary to 'cap the climax' of my comfort, is a few plugs of common tobacco." Apparently Heydenfeldt failed to send the tobacco, or Foley set his sights higher than a few plugs after all. Soon Estell appointed Foley a night guard, whereupon Foley took five hundred dollars from the prison safe and his leave, explaining in a gratuitous note that he considered the money a loan. The authorities never recaptured him.[31]

Other witnesses confirmed seeing convicts known to be serving time at San Quentin freely wandering the streets of San Francisco. The officers and guards of the prison offered in evidence a letter they had addressed a month earlier to their superiors, in which they requested a raise in pay commensurate with their "dangerous situation." One witness, the prison's part-time physician, Dr. Alfred Taliaferro, referred to the guards themselves as "desperate men" who drank too much.[32]

In the end, the 1855 Special Committee recommended accepting Estell's offer to purchase his contract because "the probability of [the convicts'] escape is so apparent to the citizens adjoining the prison, that they live in constant fear and . . . the price of real estate in the surrounding country has been materially reduced in consequence thereof."[33]

The Board of Prison Inspectors also recommended terminating the contract system. This board, which consisted of Horace Carpentier, the former prison commissioner who had objected to the railroading of a construction contract with Ferdinand Vassault; James Miller; and Richard Snowden, voiced some penological concerns as well as custodial ones. Indeed, they thought that with its crowded and unsanitary conditions, the prison actually excelled as "a place of suffering and expiation."[34]

The inspectors were concerned generally about the unpredictability of the penal process. Proclaiming that it is "the certainty of punishment . . . and not its severity that gives force and efficiency to penal laws," the board illustrated the capriciousness of the penal code: "By the existing law the larceny of $50 is punishable by death, while the higher crime of arson is punished with imprisonment not to exceed two years." Disorder in the prison, they suggested, could find some cure in the reform of a corrupt system of justice: "We . . . recommend that the criminal laws be carefully revised, that the jury system be remodeled so as to secure, if possible, some honesty in the mode of empaneling and selecting juries, and that the rule of evidence be changed so as to insure a more just and certain administration of the penal statutes."[35]

In the same paragraph the inspectors asserted that the certainty of the death penalty for particular crimes, ranging from larceny to murder, caused juries to acquit the guilty and the governor to spend an excessive amount of time reexamining cases and considering use of the pardoning power.[36]

These represented relatively advanced views at a time when the public was more concerned about protecting itself from desperate convicts than about improving criminal justice. The prison conditions themselves, in which "ignorant, stupid and submissive" inmates intermingled with "vicious" ones, reflected the same philosophy as the criminal code did, with all of its death penalties: Either people are good, or they are evil. As long as such a view prevailed, then the only solutions to the prison problem that seemed applicable were to give control to the state and to build a stronger hold.

The inspectors indeed concluded that commitment to any socially important goal such as reformation of the criminal required an end to the contract system wherein "the first object of prison discipline will be to obtain the maximum labor with the minimum cost." They warned that such a redirection would require the state to undertake considerable building expenses.

A wall seemed essential to the inspectors as well as to the neighboring public: "[Prisoners] will hardly be secured, at present, without a wall enclosing the prison grounds and invariable confinement of the prisoners within the same." If a prison failed to deprive its inmates of their freedom, then it was to no purpose: "If the wall will only serve to shut out the prisoners, instead of being as it ought to be, an impassable barrier between them and society, then its construction would be useless and extravagant," they wrote, referring to the need also to eliminate the practice of working away from prison grounds.[37]

With Estell, the prison employees, and Marin County citizens equally frightened of prisoner escape and violent retribution, the legislature agreed to the Special Committee's recommendation that the state buy Estell's contract and assume management of the State Prison. Recognizing the inspectors' concerns about safekeeping, if not their concerns about criminal justice and prisoner reformation, the legislature immediately authorized construction of a brick and stone wall.

THE STATE TAKES OVER

The new law authorized a paid, three-man Board of Directors. The first board was to be chosen by the legislature and the subsequent boards by general election; all of the directors would live at the prison and one among them would be warden, one clerk, and one president of the board. The state's new system did not last long. Less than a year after the state took control of the prison, another legislative committee appointed to examine prison affairs reported a new scandal, this time involving financial mismanagement or outright fraud, and a new round of hearings ensued. These ultimately led to a resumption of Estell's leasehold. The committee reported finding "heavy expenditures made by the State Prison Directors since the State ha[d] taken possession of the State Prison." In the seven months between June 1, 1855, and January 1, 1856, the committee found that the directors had "created obligations or claims against the State to the amount of $388,278.91."[38]

Much of the new scandal pertained, again, to prison construction; this time to the construction of the mandated wall around the prison. In its authorization to James Smiley of San Francisco, the contractor who built the wall, the legislature had specified the wall's dimensions and agreed to provide the bricks to be used in its construction. But instead of the 1,250,000 bricks a wall of the authorized size would have contained, the committee calculated that Smiley had used 1,309,605 bricks to compose the actual wall. What was more, while the legislature had mandated the use of cement as mortar, the committee found that Smiley had instead used a porous, doughy lime mixture that compromised the wall's integrity. And finally, while the plans called for a wall five hundred feet square, the committee found "utter disregard of symmetry as well as the gross violation of the law itself." Smiley had received the construction contract for the wall without competing in open bidding or using convict labor as required. Considerable testimony, technical and otherwise, followed these discoveries, which led the committee to conclude that, by returning to the lease system, the state would regain fiduciary control over the prison, if not behavioral control over the prisoners. Reverting to the lease system, the committee predicted, would enable the state to "know how much will be required for the actual support and maintenance of the State Prison, and when her expenditures will cease."[39]

Perhaps as important as the predictability of prison expenses was their

assignment to some other party. In 1855, when the state first abrogated its
ten-year contract with the prison lessee, it did so in order to instill discipline
and order into the chaos in which the desperate criminals at San Quentin
lived. The state's first board-appointed warden, John S. Love, seems to have
taken seriously the task of organizing the prison. On November 17, 1855, he
issued a set of twelve "Rules and Regulations of the California State Prison."
Five of those rules pertained to the guards' keeping of arms, and ranged from
admonishing that "no guard . . . must at any time leave his gun at more than
a distance of three feet from him" to ordering that "in case of an insurrec-
tion the Guard must . . . when necessary to fire, shout at the prisoners to
lay down, and shoot to kill if possible, but only those who are standing up
or running about." Clearly Love intended to respect his mission to end the
escapes and abate the citizens' fears and the bad publicity so predominant
during the lessee's reign. Nonetheless, during this same interval, from 1855
to 1856, the state's total prison expenditures increased from $57,992.23 to
$411,246.14. The 1856 figures represented serious financial corruption and
quickly superseded the old fears of violent prisoner rebellion.[40]

When the legislature accepted the committee's recommendation to return
to the lease system, it tacitly announced that financial austerity overrode safekeeping as the governing principle of the prison system. In a significant move,
the state did not accept the Prison Directors' plea that "two more Prison
Buildings of the same size as the present one, to enable us to keep the convicts securely . . . are required to be built immediately." Instead, in its new
five-year contract with the lessee, the legislature authorized him to erect such
buildings as necessary for the proper securing of prisoners at his own cost,
but in accordance with plans such as the new Board of State Prison Commissioners would approve.[41] This clause later caused considerable controversy
when the state used the sublessees' refusal to build the approved structures
as one reason to revoke the contract. Even though the new lease provided
up to fifteen thousand dollars per month for the safekeeping of convicts (the
lessees were actually receiving ten thousand dollars per month), the sublessees claimed that the state's attempt to foist on them responsibility for an
expensive prison complex amounted to extortion.

Also significant, in light of his previous failure, is the legislature's choice
of Estell, once again, as the lessee. Estell, who had by then been elected to
the state's assembly and had been instrumental in the election of the new

governor, Neely Johnson, was eager to regain the lease under the new terms. He duly delivered a two hundred thousand-dollar bond, though in dubious sureties, in return for the convicts' labor and ten thousand dollars per month. Clearly California was eager to transfer the financial burden of the prison to someone else, even to Estell.[42]

THE LESSEES HAVE A SECOND CHANCE

Prison conditions deteriorated further. By the time an assembly select committee examined the prison grounds in February 1857, one year after Estell resumed his contract, there were 483 prisoners sleeping in the Stones, still the sole prison building. Estell was finished. While the state advertised for a new contractor, he sublet the convicts himself. Two months later, on May 14, 1857, John F. McCauley and Lloyd Tevis took control of San Quentin as the assignees of Estell's lease. McCauley, who governed the prison, was by all accounts far more opportunistic and brutal than Estell had been. In its 1859 suit to regain the prison and exact damages, the state alleged that McCauley ignored his charge both to treat prisoners humanely and to harbor them securely. Instead, by neglecting to clothe prisoners properly, by feeding them "unwholesome and insufficient food," and by refusing to improve their quarters, McCauley created "a state of disaffection" so great that many prisoners "risk[ed] their lives in desperate attempts to escape." Although McCauley claimed the right to shoot "in cold blood" escapees or potential escapees, he also failed to pursue them once they had successfully eluded the guard.[43]

Under the conditions of the 1856 act returning prison control to private hands, the lessees this time were to pay for the "erecting of suitable buildings for the protection and security of said convicts." The legislation, however, retained for the state control over the plans and the construction schedule of those suitable buildings. In accordance with this new law, the state hired architect Miner F. Butler to develop plans and specifications for additional prison buildings. Butler, a young Georgian, had arrived in California with the Argonauts of 1849, and designed a number of institutional buildings in the new state, including the State Agricultural Pavilion and the Nevada County Courthouse. His design won the competition for the state capital in Sacramento. Butler first visited the San Quentin site in June 1856, during which time the new Board of State Prison Commissioners determined the

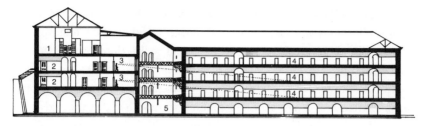

1 Females' Department
2 Officers' Rooms
3 Officer
4 Cells
5 Open Court

1. 1857 cell block plan, San Quentin. Dotted lines indicate the guard's line of sight. (Redrawn by Jamie Calhoun from the original plan in the California State Archives supplied by courtesy of the Office of the Secretary of State, Sacramento.)

exact siting and size of the proposed buildings. The board contemplated two new buildings: one a combination hospital, dining room, and female department, and the other a new cell building, deemed the more urgent need. An existing unsigned plan labeled "San Quentin" and dated 1857 shows a cell building with three tiers of forty-square-foot (four and a half by nine feet) cells, fifty-eight to a tier, all visible from the first floor.[44]

In a letter to the board dated December 29, 1857, Butler explained that he had been unable to commence construction because of a dispute between Estell and McCauley, apparently over financial liability for the project. The next month, January 1858, the board received a series of estimates evaluating Butler's plans in a move to authorize payment and initiate construction.[45]

By that time the legislature was officially considering admitting defeat at San Quentin and relocating the prison convicts entirely. Butler alluded to this possibility in his December letter, explaining that McCauley had stopped postponing new construction because of a dispute with Estell and had begun to postpone it instead because of the impending removal of the prison. The inability of the legislature to work with the sublessees proved an inducement to move the prison, as did a reassessment of the San Quentin site and years of complaints by Marin County residents. The joint legislative committee visiting the state prison reported on January 18, 1858, that San Quentin had insufficient water, no access roads, no trees of any value, spent clay, gross overcrowding, and required expensive land leveling for expansion of the facilities. A census of prisoners found ten on the roster living off of prison grounds and three completely unaccounted for. One hundred and twenty prisoners were barefoot and none had socks. Some wore pieces of gunny sacks or blankets around their feet.[46]

On the second day of the committee's visit, however, many of the prisoners sported brand new shoes. Conditions were so bad that the legislators reported massive "suffering with which death with all its terrors would be a seeming pleasurable relief." The worst feature of San Quentin to this group, though, echoing the 1855 prison inspectors' concerns, was not the cold, the lice, or the shackles, but "the long room, so called, which is in size 24' by 146' [where the prisoners] are turned loose, like so many brute animals in a corral, to stay, to sleep, the young, middle-aged, and old . . . thus rendering reform and reformation seemingly impossible."[47]

The brutal San Quentin experience and the intense frustration from working with profit-oriented lessees caused this committee to consider instituting some basic penological wisdom employed or lionized elsewhere for decades. Its recommendations included prison uniforms for warmth and comfort as well as for easy identification of escapees, removal of all female prisoners to some unspecified spot, elimination of all inhumane punishments, acquisition of books, observance of sabbath days, and, above all, the classification and segregation of prisoners. Indeed, as McCauley suspected, this committee thought such a prison program would best derive from scratch and recommended abandoning the San Quentin site in favor of an unnamed site in a "better location with a quantity of granite."[48]

The significant prison bill that passed in 1858 encompassed this committee's recommendations only in part. The act of 1858 once again removed control of the prison from private hands and, this time, also from the hands of a paid board of directors. Instead, the legislature opted for an ex-officio board consisting of the governor, the secretary of state, and the lieutenant-governor, who would serve as warden, in the hope that such a board would have less to gain from corruption than would a full-time board. This act also authorized a branch prison, to be sited and built as a replacement for the miserable San Quentin facilities. Once the state resumed control over San Quentin, however, many of the improvements the lessees had refused to enact were forthcoming. McCauley and Tevis had tried to prevent a new administration from assuming control of the prison, and when that failed, they sued the state for contract violation. While McCauley and Tevis were in court testifying that the state had exceeded its authority by hiring an architect and demanding that the lessees build expensive new quarters, the next new Board of Directors, impelled by the force of the revelations, commenced the construction of the buildings Butler had designed.[49] The suit McCauley and Tevis had brought against the state for damages finally ended in October 1860; the two shared a $275,000 settlement with Estell's widow. Even during the litigation and perhaps because of its being frequently in the news, the state completed a combination hospital, women's quarters, and dungeon, the latter offering an alternative to the flogging post. At last there was visible progress at the state prison, although it had cost many additional dollars to be finally free of the money-saving contract system.[50]

SAN QUENTIN WITHOUT CONTROVERSY

The December 31, 1860, report of the State Prison Directors at long last registered optimism about the governability of San Quentin. The directors were "gratified" to report only three escapes had occurred that year, even though the suit by McCauley and Tevis had been undecided until October. This statistic seemed to belie the sublessees' claim that the reason they had suffered so many escapes was that the continuing contract dispute led prisoners to believe they were unlawfully incarcerated. Furthermore, the directors reported that the expenses incurred had not been wasteful, but had enhanced the "comfort, cleanliness, and convenience of the officers and guards," a long-neglected group. With the prisoners gainfully employed, the directors estimated the prison could run successfully on $2,225 per month, significantly less than the $10,000 per month McCauley demanded.

Rather than risk escapes by working prisoners outside San Quentin's walls, the directors asked for a "small appropriation . . . for the purchase of material and the erection of workshops." The overcrowding worried them, but they claimed that additional cell buildings could be built "with but trifling expense to the State" because, contrary to earlier reports, "excellent quality brick is on hand." Now that the state had control of the prison, the location once again looked suitable, just as it had before the lessees and multiple scandals combined to unravel the San Quentin experiment.[51]

Another Report on State Prison Conditions, dated April 5, 1862, perpetuated this sense of hope and even officially recommended a building policy that could "enable the warden to put into practice his own wise and humane views upon [the subject of the classification of prisoners]." While this committee found conditions at San Quentin much improved, that is, the general health was good and the food sufficient, the overcrowded sleeping conditions still represented a serious evil. "Aside from considerations of health, [overcrowding] is calculated to lead to the most serious moral consequences to the prisoners." In order to ameliorate this serious state, the report recommended a twenty thousand-dollar appropriation "for the purpose of immediate erection of a building 180' by 28' for 300 convicts." This size resembled the basic dimensions of the Stones, 170 by 28 feet, a size presumably designed to hold about fifty convicts. The proposed new building contemplated at least two tiers of cells rather than just one, eliminating the evil of the first floor "long room." The twenty thousand-dollar figure suggests a jerry-built structure, however, even accounting for use of convict labor and the state's own bricks. In 1853, 140 iron doors alone would have cost more than that.[52]

Expanded facilities were necessary to relieve some of the pressure within the prison, but in the meantime, escapes continued. The 1862 report announced the grim fact that escapes, or "revolts," were common at San Quentin, and that the ensuing manhunts often ended in violence: "We are of the opinion that a larger number of prisoners has been killed in attempted revolts in the State Prison of California since the year 1850 than in all the other states aggregated."[53]

This situation continued as long as those in charge refused to take control. Soon after this report, in July of 1862, a group of up to three hundred convicts participated in a mass escape that involved the kidnapping of the warden, Lieutenant Governor John Chellis. An even larger posse hunted the group and eventually found Chellis and many of the escapees. Another such escape attempt occurred in April of 1864, and the state finally augmented its shoot-to-kill orders with an Auburn-style regimen: gray- and black-striped prison uniforms, silence, and lock-step formations. This alone may have dramatically reduced the number of prison escapes to a total of seventeen between 1865 and 1875, the year when the population of San Quentin reached one thousand.[54]

In addition to the use of prison uniforms, some essential physical improvements finally did occur at San Quentin during the first unimpeded decade of state control. By 1872, seven years after the establishment of a diligent private reform group, the California Prison Commission, changed conditions at San Quentin seemed generally healthy. The success of the changes had temporarily postponed what had once seemed urgent, the building of a branch prison. A spokesman for the Prison Commission, Reverend James Woodworth, wrote:

> A revolution has taken place in the management of the Prison [since 1858], so that order and good discipline, to as great an extent as the present system will admit of, now prevail. The prisoners are all employed at various branches of industry, at as profitable rates as, under the circumstances, could reasonably be expected. Instead of one cell-house, as then, the lower portion divided into only seven rooms, there are now three such buildings, two of them containing six tiers each, three on either side, of single cells. The rickety workshops have, within a few years, been replaced by a splendid brick structure, 258 feet in length, and four and a half stories high, costing about $150,000. This contains a fine fifty horse power steam-engine, with connections for driving machinery all through the establishment.... Immense reservoirs have been constructed . . . and arrangements have been made to insure a constant and abundant supply of pure water. And a new residence for the Warden, valued at $12,000, has just been completed. So that an almost entire renewal of the institution has taken place, and the value of the improvements has increased manyfold.[55]

Thus, by the end of the first full decade of state control, important reforms had occurred at San Quentin to make the prison a functioning, habitable place. In a young state born of exigency, it had taken years of escapes, violence, mismanagement, and overcrowding before any view of the prison as an institution actually prevailed. First, it was necessary for the state government itself to develop from an ad hoc arrangement into an institution. The lease system of the first decade had proved "seriously objectionable," failing wholly "to accomplish the great object which should be aimed at by the establishment of a State Prison, namely the certainty of punishment . . . and the moral reformation of the convict."[56] Moreover, the passing of fiscal and managerial responsibility for the prison back and forth between the prison lessee and the state during the 1850s accounted in great part for the failure to build safe, secure, and humane facilities. In turn, this failure fostered a desperation shared among guards, citizens, and prisoners alike, a despera-

2. Inmates lined up in front of the "Spanish" cell blocks, San Quentin, nineteenth century.
(Zubler Collection, San Quentin Museum Association.)

tion leading to rampant escape, to the indiscriminate slaughter of escapees, and to tight security becoming the state's main goal for the prison.

Concurrent with the improvements at San Quentin was the rise of the "New Penology," a reform movement rooted in the East. The local promoters of the New Penology, the California Prison Commission, applauded the better-managed prison and more humane conditions, but they stood steadfastly in favor of a new regime of rationalization aimed at returning the convict to society as a productive citizen. Under this new program, articulated in Cincinnati in 1870 as the "Declaration of Principles," the sorting and grading of individual prisoners and the development of distinct institutions and programs for the various scientifically characterized "types" formally

3. Jute mill at San Quentin. The manufacture of jute bags was one of the only prisoner labors to prove noncontroversial. There was virtually no private competitor. Dust permeated the air when the mill was active. (San Francisco Archives, San Francisco Public Library.)

supplanted the Auburn prescription of prison discipline, hard labor, solitary confinement, and silence once and for all.

In his praise of the San Quentin improvements in 1872, James Woodworth used such qualifying phrases as "to as great an extent as the present system will admit of" and "under the circumstances," indicating that improved conditions at San Quentin were not adequate to satisfy reformers staying abreast of post–Civil War penology. While the post-lessee State Prison did an increasingly good job of keeping prisoners inside, reformers such as Woodworth saw San Quentin as an undifferentiated institution of punishment,

rather than as a place of scientific diagnosis and reformation. By 1870 even
the former prison sublessees McCauley and Tevis had both become lifetime
members of the California Prison Commission, perhaps because their experience showed unequivocally that California needed to rationalize its penal
system.[57]

When the time finally came in the late 1870s to build a branch prison at a
new location, state prison planners were to balance the influences of the New
Penology with the unique lessons of San Quentin. Overall, San Quentin
represented the greater influence, and the new prison at Folsom bore some
resemblance to the hard labor, hard discipline regime characteristic of the
Auburn style.

2

The Building of Folsom, 1868–1910

With bars they blur the gracious moon,
And blind the goodly sun
From Oscar Wilde, "The Ballad of Reading Gaol"

California built its branch prison at Folsom during the 1870s, the heyday of the New Penology, but its construction conformed much more to the homegrown lessons of San Quentin than to those of eastern penal reformers. Nationally, the Civil War had meant a remarkable decline in imprisonment almost everywhere. A number of northern and eastern states succeeded in attaining the one-man-per-cell standard between 1860 and 1865. California, however, was not so fortunate. Not only did San Quentin's population rise from 569 in 1860 to 651 in 1865, but it did so while the young male population of the state decreased, both in absolute numbers and in proportion to the young female population.[1] Overcrowding, then, was much more jarring to penologists of the northeastern states when post-war population migration, growth, and unemployment challenged the implementation of the solitary cell ideal as well as the silent system.

Overcrowding at San Quentin and the consequent mixing of first termers and hardened criminals were of constant concern in California, but of more immediate concern to early legislators was how to create from San Quentin some kind of manageable organization. Exasperated by the management and financial fiasco of prison leasing, the California legislature had passed an act authorizing the Board of Prison Directors to find a suitable site for a "branch prison" in 1858.[2] Talk of starting anew elsewhere had commenced even earlier, dating at latest to the demise and subsequent return of the lessee system to the State Prison in 1856. No one denied that the physical plant at San Quentin was inadequate in a number of respects: there were too few cells for the prisoners; there was only a jerry-built house for the guards; the work buildings and dining hall were makeshift and shabby; the women, although there were only two or three at any given time, needed segregated quarters; and the prison wall that had caused so much scandal was, after all, a pasty mass likely to succumb to any good-sized temblor.[3] By 1858, the San Quentin site itself looked to many to be increasingly undesirable. Perhaps there was nothing to salvage there. Starting fresh elsewhere seemed at least a partial solution, but where, and with what kind of prison design and management, and with what disposition of San Quentin remained debated issues for a decade.

THE SEARCH FOR A BRANCH PRISON SITE

As early as 1856, just months before the state leased its prison to Estell for the second time, Alexander Bell, a member of the Board of Directors of the State Prison, submitted a minority report to the legislature in which he called for immediate acquisition of an additional prison site "at some point more eligible to the northern part of the State especially." Bell's major reason for wanting an additional prison was financial, reflecting the board's concerns as well. Rather than shun fiscal responsibility for the prison by returning to an inefficient leasing system, Bell argued that good business management and proper planning would turn a costly operation into a profitable one for the state. In this case, good management and proper planning required an additional prison. The small San Quentin site was "not more than sufficient on which profitably and properly to work two hundred men, half the present number of prisoners." With 150 men employed making brick, 85 men quarrying, and 30 blacksmithing, Bell calculated that San Quentin could turn a net profit of $75,212 in a year. Unemployed convicts, however, consumed the potential profit, so Bell recommended building an additional prison at another brick-making and stone-quarrying site. The profits from the convict labor at the new site would soon more than compensate the state for the $300,000 appropriation required. Moreover, if the state were to use the opportunity of a second prison to separate the short-termers from the long-termers, then it could build a less secure and therefore less expensive prison.[4]

Bell based his recommendations on fiscal rather than penological concerns. His was a dissenting opinion of a joint legislative committee that sought to abjure responsibility for the pesky prison problem by returning to the leasing system. Although his ideas may have been comparatively progressive, even the crude segregation system Bell advanced reflected frugality and not social science. In his taxonomy, long-termers were "more desperate" than short-termers and so required a more securely guarded prison. This prison, he believed, could be San Quentin with two hundred fewer convicts. If so, then the new institution for the less desperate could save money on unspecified security features. Bell proposed that inmates who would soon return to society spend their time quarrying outside the prison walls, but that those whose terms exceeded ten years spend their time inside engaged in some skilled trade such as shoemaking; apparently, he was more concerned with the close confinement of the "desperate" convicts than with rehabilitation and vocational training.[5]

Obliquely addressing Bell's suggestion, the joint committee endorsed building an additional prison only at such time as when "the number of prisoners becomes so large as to require [them] to be separated." The committee specified no way to identify that number and, in fact, observed, "The present building at San Quentin is already filled to its utmost capacity, there being now four convicts in each cell, and about one hundred and fifty thrown together in one room." Postponing for some unknown time a prison to relieve the San Quentin facilities and rejecting entirely the abandonment of San Quentin, "considering the amount already expended," the committee concluded, "The most advisable course for the State to pursue, is again to revert to the contract, or leasing, system. . . ."[6]

Accordingly, the state did not heed the Bell suggestion, but instead temporarily returned control of the prison to lessees. The notion of a branch prison, however, continued to gain adherents. San Quentin simply had too little space for all the convicts to live and work in. When the lessees proved to be uncooperative once again, legislators began discussing a new prison in earnest. Less than two years after a similar committee had easily dismissed any proposal to relinquish the San Quentin site, the joint committee of the legislature, visiting the facility on January 18, 1858, could find no reason to continue operating a prison there at all. This new committee recommended a permanent removal to a better location. While improvements at San Quentin were eventually to prevent its abandonment or even its being eclipsed, this committee's devastating report gave no reason for hope. The report led to the passage on April 26, 1858, of "An Act for the Government of the State Prison Convicts, and to provide for the location of a Branch State Prison," authorizing a search to proceed for a suitable second site. The act left it to the Board of Prison Directors to assess suitable locations.[7]

The features of San Quentin's location observers most frequently blamed for the institution's malfunctioning were an inadequate amount of level land for expanding the prison plant; an exhausted supply of state-owned clay for the production of bricks; an extreme isolation that allowed escaped convicts to disappear into the woods or the bay; and poor water and soil conditions that made prison self-sufficiency impossible. These were the exact deficiencies the state sought to eliminate in its next choice of a prison location. A 360-acre site near Folsom, a town in the Sierra foothills, was among the first the legislators identified. In a senate special committee report submitted on April 16, 1859, they observed that such a location along the American River northeast of Sacramento provided "immense quantities of granite" for the profitable employment of prisoners on prison grounds. They also noted the abundance, year-round, of water, land, and water power for manufactures. A prison at the Folsom site, they believed, could correct the financial shortcomings of the San Quentin location and be a self-paying, if not entirely self-sufficient, institution.[8]

As for the prison program for which these solons sought granite, water, land, and water power, they suggested that solitary confinement in combination with congregate labor constituted the "best system." In this embrace of the Auburn solitary confinement system, they ignored any special need to grade and separate the kinds of felons in either prison, and in this they contradicted the committee immediately preceding them in 1858. Instead, they recommended a policy of removing prisoners with terms of two years or less from the state system and placing them in county jails. This would presumably eliminate some of the undesirable interaction between hardened convicts and reclaimable ones and, more important, it would substantially diminish the state prison population and, therefore, the need to build more cells.[9]

After the passage of the 1858 authorizing act, the state resumed permanent responsibility for San Quentin. This eventually resulted in some necessary improvements in the physical plant and in the state's ability to control management there as well.[10] The visible signs of progress in the existing prison allowed the legislature to defer action on the branch prison; in fact, a decade elapsed before the state officially returned to the project. In the meantime, those interested, officially or otherwise, in penology and prisons nurtured competing conceptions of a branch prison. In general, legislators, prison directors, and newspaper editorial writers favored a place where the Auburn discipline of labor, isolation, and silence could flourish. California had really not tested this system, although increased discipline at San Quentin had proven comparatively successful; many Californians, therefore, were not yet prepared to abandon what had become the standard prison model. These adherents sought a quarrying site like that at Folsom or a rival site at Rocklin in Placer County, and, in March of 1868, a decade after the original authorization of a branch prison, the legislature voted to buy one of those two.[11] An official inspection of both sites led to the purchase of the Folsom site on June 30, 1868, from the Natoma Water and Mining Company for a sum of fifteen thousand dollars in convict labor, billed at fifty cents per day.[12]

Opposition to a new Auburn-style prison came from important reform activists, and, along with some physical improvements at San Quentin, this delayed prison construction until 1874. During the ten years between the 1858 and 1868 branch prison acts the California Prison Commission had formed under the leadership of James Woodworth, a Presbyterian minister who spent considerable time at San Quentin visiting with the prisoners and observing conditions. Organized in 1865, the commission's express purpose was the emulation of the "Prison Aid Associations of the East . . . having in view the objects contemplated by such associations elsewhere." Those objects were promulgated five years later as the "Declaration of Principles" of the National Congress on Penitentiary and Reformatory Discipline, held in Cincinnati in October 1870. This declaration comprised thirty-seven principles that together defined the New Penology.[13] With them in hand, Woodworth used the opportunity of a hiatus between authorizing a branch prison, finding a site, and appropriating building funds to attempt to persuade the California legislature to experiment with post–Civil War penological innovations.

The New Penology was basically a reform platform designed to correct the weaknesses in the Auburn solitary, silent system of hard labor. New Penologists, such as the author of the thirty-seven principles, Enoch Wines, had studied the New York system and found it wanting, especially for the younger, less hardened criminals. They saw it as punitive, nonreformatory, and oblivious to the needs of those individual inmates not yet dedicated to a life of crime. Very much environmental determinists, the reformers believed that a prison could compensate for deficiencies in a young criminal's upbringing if it were properly designed, professionally staffed, and offered generous rewards for good behavior. From these principles arose practical solutions: 1) the reformatory, a school-like institution rather than a fortress-like one; 2) civil servants rather than political appointees as reformatory personnel; and 3) the indeterminate sentence, where, within a set range of a minimum and maximum term, the inmate could be adjudged rehabilitated and then set free. New York, again, was a pioneer in applying these new penological principles, and that state's reformatory at Elmira opened in 1876, a model for all.[14]

Woodworth and the California Prison Commission tirelessly advocated these principles in California. In his 1871–72 report, Woodworth announced that the organization had submitted a bill to the legislature employing the language of the New York bill that had authorized Elmira. The commission's bill, if passed, would have established a reformatory at San Quentin, leaving the main institution relieved of some of its population and adaptable to the Auburn system. Sections two and five proposed a separate institution outside the main San Quentin walls with a capacity to house no fewer than four hundred first offenders under the age of twenty-five. There they were to have required school time of at least two hours a day and, although no indeterminate sentence was proposed, the inmates were to be allowed to earn good-time credits to shorten their sentences.[15]

The legislature considered the bill, but when the assembly committee to which it had been referred changed the whereabouts of the proposed reformatory from San Quentin to Folsom, Woodworth withdrew his support of it. He wrote, "the granite quarries in the deep canyon above Folsom—with the confined limits, and with the intense heat prevailing there in the summer, might, perhaps, answer as a place for the *punishment* of a limited number of the more hardened and robust convicts," but, he argued, it should not for a moment be considered a suitable site for a reformatory. He and his group resolutely opposed the branch prison idea altogether, in great measure because other states with larger populations had only one prison, and "it would be rather humiliating for us, so early in our history . . . to confess the need of two such institutions."[16] A reformatory at San Quentin was the proper, or eastern, way to address the overcrowding and the congregating together of all types of prisoners, Woodworth asserted.

The legislature shelved any movement on either a branch prison or reformatory until 1874, but when it did reconsider the subject it was in very practical terms. A joint committee inspecting San Quentin in February of 1874 discovered 941 prisoners sharing 444 cells and eight rooms, which amounted to less than two hundred cubic feet per inmate. The committee members pronounced that the "established laws of physiology and hygiene . . . require that a healthy man should have at the very least 500 cubic feet of ventilated space." Based on the objective force of these figures, the joint committee resolved "that the interests of the State and society will be served by the establishment of a Branch State Prison," and that year the legislature authorized the first $175,000 appropriation for building another similar institution at Folsom.[17]

Overcrowded conditions at San Quentin had never permitted the practice there of the Auburn system of solitary confinement, and some officials directly responsible for California's state prison still wanted to emulate this first element of New York's system. In 1879, the year before the Branch Prison opened, the warden and resident director of San Quentin, James A. Johnson, reported to the Board of Prison Directors that, "but for a defection in the cell buildings and want of room, [we] would have to-day exactly the present New York system."[18]

Johnson, also the state's lieutenant-governor, was one of California's more enlightened prison managers. He was an easterner, born in South Carolina in 1929 and educated in Philadelphia at the Jefferson Medical School. He arrived in California in 1853 and served in the state assembly prior to his election as lieutenant-governor. In his articulate 1879 report, Johnson also suggested how California might correct its lingering deficiency: "To enable us to adopt [the Auburn] system entirely we must have cell room sufficient to prevent the doubling up of prisoners." Above all, urged Johnson, prisoners must have space and the chance to repent and grow, for "every man has within him a germ of goodness."[19]

This desire to realize fully the New York system in California became the state's fundamental goal in authorizing a new branch prison rather than a reformatory at Folsom. State officials were mindful of the embarrassment of San Quentin and wanted to rectify matters by trying again at Folsom. Like Woodworth, the legislature and prison officials used eastern standards to assess the California institutions, but, unlike the easterners who developed those standards, these Californians were not yet ready to declare the Auburn system obsolete. They first wanted to try it and excel in it. In Johnson's words, "As soon as the Folsom Prison is opened, which may be any time after the 1st of January next, a trifling outlay of money will prepare the necessary room to place each prisoner in a cell to himself. . . . Ours may then rank among the highest and best institutions for the suppression of crime and the reformation of criminals."[20] Ironically, at Folsom solitary confinement was to become an implement of punishment rather than reformation.

BUILDING THE BRANCH PRISON

While changes were looming in the management of prison affairs, construction proceeded on the Branch Prison at Folsom. As at San Quentin, contract fraud and disputes, underappropriations, and site and design controversies all characterized the initial work of building Folsom. The state's first contractor, Michael Miles, hired under the 1874 legislation to build the first 168-cell block at Folsom, abandoned his work of clearing the land in September 1875, after having been paid an advance of seventy-nine thousand dollars and completing no cells. This resulted in litigation that the state lost; the court awarded a contract assignee of Miles a thirty-four thousand-dollar settlement.[21] No further appropriations for Folsom were forthcoming while the state repaired fire damage at San Quentin in 1876, and work at the Branch Prison stopped.

By 1878, San Quentin was overflowing with more than 1,400 inmates, and the legislature once again turned its attention to Folsom. Reviewing the first set of Folsom plans, no longer extant, the solons considered the buildings as drawn unnecessarily expensive. They hired a well-known institutional archi-

4. *Cell block inside of Folsom prison walls, nineteenth century. (San Francisco Archives, San Francisco Public Library.)*

tect, A. A. Bennett, to revise the original plans and this time provide for 328 seven- by nine-foot cells, to accommodate 328 prisoners.[22] The main features of this prison plan addressed the known design deficiencies of San Quentin: 1) Folsom was to have a massive, granite cellhouse surrounding the ventilated cell blocks, with no cells having direct access to the outside, as they did at San Quentin; 2) at Folsom, the entire prison was to be a continuous, U-shaped series of connected buildings so that prisoners traveling between their cells, the administration area, and the dining room were never to step outside as they had to do at San Quentin; and 3) a thick wall and gun towers were to surround the prison grounds and provide the external security required without encountering another doughy wall, such as that which mocked San Quentin. The wall, however, was to come last, when the state could afford an adequate appropriation. These design features were all intended to achieve one principal penological end: the safekeeping of prisoners.[23]

To effect Bennett's plans, the 1878 legislature appropriated a net sum of $205,495 and let the contract out for bid. Contractor Dennis Jordan offered the lowest bid, at $161,000, and he won the contract in July of 1878. Jordan was to have completed his work within fifteen months, but he had difficulty getting credit to buy machinery and paying his workers, so that by May of 1879, it seemed that he had entirely abandoned the work, with only 44 of the 328 cells completed. The Board of Directors at that time assumed responsibility for completing the work, but Jordan filed official charges against them and the architect, Bennett, to keep his contract. Jordan claimed that Bennett, who had overseen his work, had harassed him and his workers and had insisted on his using more expensive construction techniques than necessary. The state's construction superintendent confirmed Jordan's story. Jordan wanted an additional forty thousand dollars to finish his contract, insisting that it was inappropriate for the board to take charge.[24]

The joint committee investigating the request recommended making the appropriation, although some members dissented. In an aside, some brought up the issue of Folsom being a breeding ground for malaria and questioned the notion of proceeding at all. Although this was less than a ringing endorsement for the project, the legislature passed Jordan's forty thousand-dollar appropriation in 1880 "for speedy completion of the branch prison." The next year, the state appropriated an additional nine thousand dollars for the same purpose.[25]

In March of 1880, Thomas C. Pockman became superintendent of the construction at Folsom, and on July 15, 1880, he became the prison's first warden. Although Pockman protested that it was not yet ready for habitation, on July 26 the Branch Prison officially opened to receive 44 inmates transferred from San Quentin. By October of that year, he had received enough transfers to make the prison population total 211, less 1 pardoned and 1 escaped convict.[26] Folsom was soon to become the destination for "hardened" criminals. The first Folsom inmates, however, were statistically somewhat younger and less vicious than those who stayed behind at San Quentin. Of these first 211, about 63 percent were serving their first term, and about 56 percent were under thirty years old. Only 10 of the first Folsom prisoners were fifty years old or older, and none was older than fifty-six. About 20 percent of the first prisoners were serving time for violent crimes, such as assault, manslaughter, rape, and murder. More than 27 percent of San Quentin's prisoners were similarly charged. Most of the remainder had committed theft of some degree. Eighty-four percent were serving terms of ten years or less, compared to less than 81 percent of San Quentin's inmates.

5. Prisoners laboring in the yard of the Folsom quarry. The siting committee considered the Folsom location appropriate for the prison in part because it could be quarried. (San Francisco Archives, San Francisco Public Library.)

Only 2 inmates, less than 1 percent, were serving life sentences, compared to 106, or 7 percent, in San Quentin.[27]

Pockman immediately put most of the convicts to work completing the construction and replacing the paid free laborers, as the legislature had required. Granite from the Folsom quarry was the main prison material, and the prisoners had to excavate and dress the stone as well as complete the detail work. In his first report as warden to the board, Pockman praised the conduct and work of the prisoners. He wrote, "They have been orderly, faithful to their work, and obedient to the rules."[28]

The prisoners were so orderly, in fact, that construction of a prison wall, intended as a second-phase addition, was delayed for years. Pockman, a reputed martinet, had reluctantly received prisoners at the incomplete site

6. Prisoners dressing stone at the Folsom quarry. Quarrying became part of a general prison labor controversy. In the nineteenth century, professional stone dressers objected to prisoners undertaking this work. (San Francisco Archives, San Francisco Public Library.)

and had intended to maintain discipline there temporarily with a series of manned gun platforms. The only "wall" around Folsom in 1880 consisted of an imaginary boundary line connecting the gun posts. Pockman called this the "deadline," and issued a standing order to the guards to shoot any prisoner crossing the line. This psychological boundary was apparently effective, for Folsom had few reported escape attempts until 1883, after Pockman's term, when there were eleven successful ones. That year the legislature appropriated seven thousand dollars for the purchase of material to build a wall around Folsom, but, in fact, a return of order meant the wall did not get built even then. From 1890 to 1898 the number of escapes totaled nineteen, an average of two per year.[29]

7. *Guard towers succeeded makeshift gun platforms around the grounds of Folsom prison. (San Francisco Archives, San Francisco Public Library.)*

AN ADMINISTRATIVE REFORM VICTORY, A PRISON LABOR FAILURE

California's New Penologists, as represented most articulately by Woodworth and the California Prison Commission, lost the reformatory issue in favor of a branch prison at Folsom. Nonetheless, they won a victory on a different point in 1879 that promised to make California a leader among progressive states. Reverend Woodworth's commission proposed the elimination of the Board of Prison Directors as constituted since 1858: an ex-officio group in residence at San Quentin, where the lieutenant governor of the state also served as warden. Among the many reasons advanced for a change were that the lieutenant governor had other duties requiring him to be in Sacramento and that qualifications for office did not necessarily apply to running a prison. Article VI of the New Penologists' "Declaration of Principles" supplied the basic argument for making such administrative changes: "The two master forces opposed to the reform of the prison systems of our several states are political appointments and a consequent instability of administration." [30]

Eliminating politicians from prison management, in other words, seemed essential to the achievement of any prison reform. In keeping with this principle, a number of eminent eastern penologists authored an article for the new state constitution of New York, proposing an unpaid lay board of directors whose members would serve ten-year terms. The idea was that an unpaid board would have less to gain from graft, and also that ten-year terms would scatter the appointments through numerous gubernatorial administrations. In his 1872 report, Woodworth noted that the commission had adapted the New York language for California and presented to the Sacramento legislature as a potential constitutional amendment a bill to establish a similar board. [31]

The bill failed to pass that year, but the commission dutifully lobbied for the bill in the next legislative session. Although this time Governor Newton Booth offered his support for it, it once again went down to defeat. The legislature did, however, appoint a joint committee to investigate prison management and make recommendations, which it did in 1874; the committee's report strongly favored the nonpartisan principles expressed in the commission's bill. The 1876 legislature passed a bill reconstituting the board. But under this law the governor, in consultation with the senate, was to appoint by January 1880 three directors for staggered four-year terms, each director receiving eight dollars a day when performing official duties. This board was to appoint the prison warden and other officers. Central to this law was the provision that the board would provide industry for the convicts and not contract for their labor inside or outside of the prison. The act was silent as to the kinds of work or industries the board might develop on the prison grounds, but it did allow the inmates to pocket up to 10 percent of their earnings, if the board should so choose. [32]

This was a victory in principle for the New Penology, yet it underscored a strange-bedfellow relationship in California, in which angry antigovernment activists teamed with the better-government reformers for more complete administrative changes. Contracting of prison labor had been ceaselessly controversial in the state, with many free laborers and their representatives crying out against what they called the unfair competition of prison labor. [33] After taking control of prison management from the lessees in 1858, the state had implemented labor reform that continued to permit the contracting of prison labor, but which required all work to be done within prison walls. By 1875 contractors employed San Quentin prisoners in privately constructed workshops on prison grounds in the following ways: 115 convicts worked on the prison grounds for Stone and Hayden, saddle and harness makers; 206 convicts worked there for Merriam and Cole, furniture manufacturers; and 100 inmates made boots and shoes for A. W. Baldwin.[34]

This 1858 change in prison labor laws had silenced the local complaints about prisoners working away from their place of incarceration, but it incensed the vociferous Californians who jealously guarded all work opportunities. Just as free, white, male Californians wanted to eliminate competition from Chinese labor, they also wanted an end to competition from prison labor. Addressing this demand in 1873, the legislature passed a minimum charge for convict labor of fifty cents per day.[35] Nonetheless, resentful Californians continued to want a total ban on these contracts, and such resentment only increased through the 1870s, as mining stocks collapsed and hard times exaggerated the economic disparity between workers and capitalists. By 1879 representatives of the state's working classes joined with reformers to draft a new state constitution.

Legislative calls for a new constitution had occurred as early as 1857. The original constitution proved vague at best in defining governmental organization, in apportioning representation, and in limiting legislative powers of taxation and expenditures. Suspicion of politicians ran deep by 1879; continual stories of opportunism and graft offended both workers and reformers. To prevent future governmental excesses, including what many considered excessive gubernatorial use of unrestricted pardoning power, 152 delegates convening for 156 working days authorized the new constitution. This was a massive and detailed document, leaving as little as possible to official interpretation.[36]

Article X of California's new constitution contained the main provisions of the Prison Commission's administration reform proposals, which had passed in principle during the legislative session of 1876, and it included a provision abolishing contract prison labor after January 1, 1882. As a substitute for the latter, the constitution allowed for prisoner manufacture of items not already made by free mechanics and items to be used by the state. A bill passed in 1880 to effect these new constitutional clauses; it provided for a five-member Board of Directors, with staggered terms of ten years each, which would appoint the warden and supervise the separate prisons at San Quentin and Folsom. Also, the board would be responsible for the creation and success of prison industries, whatever those were to be, and for recommending prisoners for pardon.[37]

Woodworth and the California Prison Commission believed the creation of this board to be a great victory. By inaugurating this reform in prison administration, California seemed for a brief time to take a penological lead among the states. Even Enoch Wines, the acknowledged leader of the New Penology movement, praised California's reforms and Woodworth. In his essay, *The State of Prisons and Child-Saving Institutions in the Civilized World*, Wines wrote that California's new constitution "contains one article . . . which places her in the forefront of all States on the North American continent in the matter of prison reform."[38] He referred to the new centralized management of a nonpolitical prison board.

The first directors the governor appointed were five "gentlemen of intelligence, integrity, and well established business character": Augustus H. Chapman, from Chico; William F. McNutt, M.D., from San Francisco; Wallace Everson, from Oakland; George W. Schell, from Modesto; and Jacob H. Neff, from Colfax.[39] The duties they assumed were difficult, if not impossible: they were to preside over the completion of the Branch Prison at Folsom, oversee management of two separate prisons, and develop prison industries not competitive with free labor and on a low budget to provide work for convicts and to achieve self-supporting institutions.

By 1883, in spite of reported improvements at San Quentin, such as the installation of gaslights and progress in the completion of Folsom, this first, well-intended Board of Directors had infuriated the labor representatives in the legislature. That year a senate committee investigating several charges against the directors concluded, "[They] have been grossly negligent in the performance of the duties assigned to them, having taken favors, spent more money than authorized, and kept poor records, and this committee recommended that Governor George Stoneman take appropriate action to dismiss them," which he did.[40]

The directors greatest offenses were, in fact, unconnected to political favor, but instead to the sensitive (and xenophobic) issue of labor competition. Chief among the directors' crimes were purchasing machinery made in England for use at San Quentin; selling in the private sector convict-made goods that the state refused to buy; and using Chinese convict labor in San Quentin's new jute bag factory, when the new constitution strictly forbade any Chinese employment. Although this Board of Prison Directors stood for important New Penology-type changes, it actually served more at the behest of the nativists than of the reformers, the two groups who, together, had created it.[41] Succeeding boards continued to run afoul of free labor's demands.

CONVICT TREATMENT AT FOLSOM

If Folsom was to implement the Auburn system, it needed to house industry for the employment of the inmates. In spite of the new constitutional restrictions on the use of convict labor, this initially seemed to be no problem. The Natoma Water Company, later known as the Folsom Water Company and later still as the Sacramento Electric, Gas and Railway Company, had deeded the state the land for the branch prison in return for fifteen thousand dollars worth of convict labor, at fifty cents per convict per day, to build a canal and dam for the company's use. Also, the convicts were to build a powerhouse to generate electricity for the prison's use and a reservoir to supply the prison. Disputes about the implementation of these agreements occurred and consequent delays in the work and improvements lasted until 1888.[42] Because of the constitutional prohibitions against contract labor and subsequent laws prohibiting competitive prison industries, the only paying work left for the convicts was quarrying the enormous mass of granite, and the Irish stonecutters' union protested that.[43] The wardens, prison directors, and, reportedly, the prisoners shared the frustration over this situation. Infighting within the prison was one manifestation of this frustration.

To the disappointment of the Board of Prison Directors, Thomas Pockman, who had kept such good control of the prisoners, stepped down as Folsom's warden in 1881, and John McComb assumed the job. A general in the National Guard and a veteran newspaper man, McComb managed to complete the construction of the main prison buildings, improve ventilation within its stifling cells, and start a prison farm. He also permitted some disciplinary measures that were to bring him notoriety. On visiting Folsom in July 1887, the Board of Prison Directors interviewed, among others, twelve inmates held in "solitary," or "dungeon," cells. The physical condition of these prisoners horrified Director A. J. Filcher, who indicted McComb for cruelty in a subsequent newspaper interview. On the defense, McComb demanded and got a full hearing before the board. Whereas Filcher had learned that the men in the dungeon were unwashed, unexercised, poorly fed, and left endlessly in darkened cells, McComb denied mistreatment. He claimed that he kept in solitary confinement only those men who threatened to escape or to kill, insisting that security was at issue and not punishment. In fact, according to McComb, he had eliminated flogging and "the shower," the latter being a punishment in which guards stripped the recalcitrant inmate naked, tied him to a cross, and beat him from his face to his genitalia with the force of water from a high-pressure hose.

Preparatory to McComb's hearings, the prison directors asked the secretary of state to inquire of the wardens of such eastern prisons as Cherry Hill (New Jersey), Sing Sing, Joliet, and Leavenworth as to their practices of punishment. He reported that all used solitary confinement, among other forms of punishment. Unlike some of the eastern dungeon cells, which were especially constructed as punishment cells, Folsom's solitary cells were identical to the regular cells, but with their ventilation grates closed. Indeed, McComb admitted that prisoners in confinement had lately had no exercise, but that was presumably temporary. During roof renovations, the prison building had several overhead escape routes accessible to these desperate prisoners. It was true, he also admitted, that several of Folsom's prisoners bore shackles during their confinement, but this was strictly to prevent escapes. One of these shackle devices was the "Oregon boot," a metal clamp or vise placed on the offender's foot and tightened slowly. Even that was not entirely foolproof. One convict so shackled and confined for more than nineteen months was William Schmidt, serving his second term for robbery. The *San Francisco Chronicle* reported, "Schmidt is regarded as the champion handcuff and leg-iron breaker in the country. . . . The only means adopted to secure [the Oregon boot] on Schmidt's person is to fill the interstices of the boot with fine emery powder which cuts any wire or file that he may use to free himself from the manacle."[44]

McComb's hearings proved rancorous, with Director Filcher proclaiming cruelty, while the remaining directors applauded McComb's strict and humane treatment of convicts. Indeed, the board voted confidence in McComb and returned him to his job. The board also recommended removal of Folsom's most desperate criminals to San Quentin, where the wall would help keep them under control without resort to solitary confinement. After this vote McComb chose to leave Folsom and he eventually assumed wardenship of San Quentin.

Charles Aull succeeded McComb in 1887 and proved to be one of the most brutal wardens in the prison's history. Aull, who had been a Pinkerton detective and who had served in various capacities at San Quentin, reportedly added new tortures to the guards' repertoire. These, according to an in-house Folsom history, included "tricing" and the "derrick." In the former, the guards attached an offending convict to a beam by his thumbs and then caused the beam to be lifted until the convict's toes barely reached the ground. The guards then left the victim to suffer for hours in this position. In the latter, a handcuffed convict was raised with his feet above his head and left. Aull retained his post through the end of the century, though, without provoking special cruelty investigations. Under Aull's regime there were virtually no prisoner rebellions, escapes, or brutality scandals. Officially, Folsom was peaceful.[45]

SYSTEM REFORMS

Through the end of the century few changes occurred in the operations of either of the state prisons, but several reforms on the outside affected California's penal system. Principal among these changes were the juvenile reform schools that replaced the prisons for youthful felons. The New Penologists had promoted a penal program that required the construction of multiple prison facilities in order to segregate criminals by age, sex, manner of employment, and degree of reformability, as determined through application of scientific criteria. While California legislators were not inclined to ease the frustrations inherent in the paradoxical missions of the state prisons, they did finally take steps in 1889 to remove juvenile offenders from San Quentin and Folsom. As the quasi-official California Prison Commission had been demanding since 1865, and as the official California State Penological Commission had recommended in 1887, the legislature finally authorized the establishment of two reform schools, one in the northern part of the state and one in the south. Accordingly, the Whittier State School in the Los Angeles area opened in 1891 for boys between eight and eighteen years of age. The Preston School of Industry in Ione opened for a similar population in 1894.

These new institutions, under separate board of trustee administrations, relieved Folsom and San Quentin of their underage charges.[46]

Having created juvenile reform schools, the state steadfastly resisted other elements of the New Penology program, such as the indeterminate sentence, the grading and separating of adult convicts, and productive forms of prison labor. Separating the juvenile offenders from the adult offenders, in fact, probably made it easier to avoid reform of harsh conditions within the prisons.

By the late nineteenth century, many reformers became increasingly attracted to nonprison options for deserving adult felons. Even though the ranks of professional law-enforcement officers and prosecuting attorneys grew in the latter part of the century, reforms to the legal system had been inadequate to correct some of the excessive sentences that the 1855 prison inspectors had damned as unjust. According to some studies, there developed with this expertise an ability to maneuver creatively within the existing system. Plea bargaining, for example, came to be an option during this time, at least in Alameda County (Oakland). Some of this bargaining was implicit, rather than explicit, as criminals who agreed to plead guilty began to receive lighter sentences.[47]

Parole, too, offered an important, nonprison option that attracted reformers who were unable to change conditions within the prisons. Since 1864, California had offered "good-time" credits to felons not sentenced to life as a way to shorten their prison terms.[48] The good-time system, administered by prison officials, allowed prisoners a reduction in their sentences for good behavior. Reformers, however, desired a more rational system, administered externally. New Penologists had endorsed "conditional pardons," but it was their Progressive-era successors who, nationwide, endorsed parole as a way to relieve prison overcrowding, to bring professional skills to bear on the rehabilitation of receptive convicts, and to offer the convicts inducement to change. An important study of its origins in California, however, shows that parole there only belatedly served rehabilitative ends.[49] In a state where sentences continued to be unpredictable and out of proportion to the crime, governors continued to spend a tremendous portion of their time reviewing requests for pardons.[50] Parole seemed to offer an alternative solution. In 1889, the state instituted parole for the juvenile felons incarcerated at Preston and Whittier.[51] Finally, in 1893, in face of considerable public opposition, Governor Henry Markham, the legislation's key advocate, signed the state's first parole bill for adult first offenders not convicted of murder. The already overburdened Board of Prison Directors assumed the responsibility for administering parole.[52]

During the remaining years of the century, the board actually paroled very few prisoners. Statistics from December 1906 show that the directors had paroled only 233 of the 720 eligible prisoners, or one-third the percentage of prisoners the state of Illinois paroled annually. The California board believed the law unpopular and, possibly, even unwise.[53]

THE GREAT ESCAPE FROM FOLSOM

While the legislature was stymied on prison reform, tedium within Folsom proved unrelenting. Manufacturing items for in-house use did occupy some of the state convicts' time, but most of the workshops, materials, and skilled personnel belonged to San Quentin. At Folsom in 1898, where "the departments are operated entirely by convict labor under the supervision and management of officers and employees," in-house products included "ice, tin ware, boots, shoes, clothing and under clothing, beds and bedding," and the small agricultural area produced "enough milk to supply the prison . . . hay, vegetables of various kinds, fruits, pork, bacon and ham." With occasional exceptions, the quantity of production was "sufficient for the uses of the prison," then housing some nine hundred inmates. Moreover, prisoners conducted "the entire clerical work" with no additional "bookkeepers, phonographers, typewriters, photographers, [or] draughtsmen" being employed.[54] Even with this activity outside the quarry, Folsom prisoners averaged only four hours of work per day.

The Prison Directors and the warden begged for some relief from this idleness, in part to address their budgetary constraints as well as to engage the inmates. The feared Warden Aull, writing in 1895, asserted, "The cry of 'competition with free labor' is ridiculous," and he proposed diversifying industries to make the men and the prison self-sufficient. "These men have to live," he reminded the legislature.[55] That year, in fact, the state senate considered a bill to establish a vocational furniture factory at Folsom, but it went down to easy defeat.[56] In 1898, Aull's report to a joint legislative prison committee pleaded for additional provisions to make it possible for more in-house production; with "proper machinery and facilities" inmates could make "clothing of all kinds, boots, shoes, iron beds . . . as well as other articles in which labor is the prime cost of the item."[57]

The legislature continued to turn a deaf ear to all attempts to make Folsom anything other than a custodial institution. Grim discipline prevailed to keep the men in line. In its 1902 report, the California Prison Commission announced that Folsom inmates were subject to hours of agonizing physical constriction in a cruel disciplinary device known as a straight jacket. The commission reported that some men were killed or permanently deformed by use of this punishment. The straight jacket, unlike the shirt designed to restrain an out-of-control asylum inmate, was a canvas girdle made strictly for the purpose of torturing prisoners simply and effectively. This device, reportedly invented and already outlawed in England, immobilized its victims, as their bound limbs grew numb and, with their strangled lungs, they gasped for each breath. Prisoners designated to suffer the straight jacket first stripped naked, then the administering guards placed the device so that it extended from the length of the victim's torso to his legs. Digging their knees into the victim's back to force him to expel air, the guards then laced the device as tightly as possible and left the victim on the floor to suffer for hours, or even days at a time, occasionally retightening the ties.[58]

With this exposé, the Board of Prison Directors issued a pronouncement abolishing the use of the straight jacket, and early in 1903 the legislature sent a special committee to investigate the charge that state prisoners were subject to cruel and unusual punishments, especially to investigate the use of the straight jacket.[59] The committee found that Folsom Warden Thomas Wilkinson, who had succeeded Aull in 1899, indeed permitted various cruelties, and the character of the prison suffered from poor food, opium traffic, inadequate clothing, and cruel punishments.

Almost to underscore the Folsom revelations came a notorious escape. On July 27, 1903, fourteen men, led by a prisoner named R. M. Gordon, used contraband dynamite and knives to overpower the guards, take the armory, and eventually effect their escape. Newspapers were full of frightening reports with headlines like "People of Mountain Town in Terror," until dispatched soldiers and posses captured each escapee, one by one. One recaptured prisoner, Jack Black, articulated the motivations for escape in an article he sold to the *San Francisco Bulletin*: "We saw there was no hope, no chance. Nothing but violence, murder, could touch those officers over us. Talk of a desperate break began to take shape."[60]

Not all analysts blamed the escape on prison conditions, however. Reporting to the governor one month after the escape, the Board of Prison Directors cited a number of evils responsible for the break, including the "sickly sentimentality" over harsh prison discipline that prevailed in the previous year's straight-jacket hearings. Evincing no such sentiment themselves, the directors unanimously opined, "It is the duty of all officers and guards to prevent the escape of convicts at every risk," including the risk of killing hostages or themselves.[61]

Indeed, the straight jacket had not disappeared from Folsom. Jack Black, in somewhat later memoir, reported that he experienced the punishment on his recapture:

> The straitjacket reached from my neck to my knees. It was a long, broad piece of plain canvas which laced up the back. There were pockets sewed into the inside of the canvas into which my arms were put. . . .
>
> I was then pushed over on my face. [The guard] laced the jacket up the back. He laced it up with a soft, stout rope, as even as a shoelace. . . .
>
> I remember distinctly now that my fingers and hands were tingling, numb, dead before he finished lacing me up. When he had finished he turned me over on my back.
>
> I can't describe the sensation now. I never could.
>
> I got to a stage where I couldn't breathe. Every time I breathed it seemed that knives were penetrating to my lungs. It got to a certain pitch—I didn't think one could suffer so much.[62]

OPTIONS FOR CHANGE

Reviewing the causes of the 1903 escape, the Board of Prison Directors identified two major improvements that Folsom required: One, the congregate system, "pleasant though it may be for the more hardened criminal," needed to end; and, two, there needed to be a prison wall. In the latter recommendation, the committee echoed its immediate predecessor, which claimed that the lack of a prison wall contributed to the harsh conditions and prisoners' restlessness.[63]

In 1903 the board announced it had ordered the acquisition of granite to start building a prison wall, trusting that the legislature would soon allocate the funds for completion. Nevertheless, the first biennial report of the new state oversight body, the State Board of Charities and Corrections, lamented that no such construction had commenced by July 1904.[64] Archibald Yell, the new Folsom warden, explained that the prison population had increased 20 percent since 1903, and the need for new cell buildings strained the construction capacity of the prisoners. Although by 1907 the legislature had appropriated $168,000 for both cell building and wall construction, Yell could only say the workers had prepared the wall's foundation. By 1909 no work had been done on the new cell building, although the prison population hovered at about one thousand, but the south line of the wall "was pretty well underway." Construction even then was occasional. The prison wall at Folsom that was intended to ease tensions and provide a means of control other than the threat of brutality was in fact not finished until 1922.[65]

Only intimidation could make a prison work in absence of a wall, all prison administrators seemed to agree, especially given the evils of the universally denounced congregate system. Yet it would take the dedication of funds for building cells to effect any other system. Initiating an effective parole system began to intrigue some legislators. An assembly committee appointed in 1905 to suggest corrective measures damned the congregate system, as had all observers for the previous fifty years, and suggested a solution other than the unpopular one of building more prisons using the same system: "We believe that there is a method by which this congested condition of the prisons could be relieved, and that instead of building more and larger prisons, we should have some system of releasing the prisoners. . . . We refer to parole."[66]

As California entered the new century, the state's prisons looked slightly different than they had in 1880, when Folsom opened. Juvenile offenders no longer mingled in the state prisons with older felons. An unpaid Board of Prison Directors oversaw the operations of both prisons. Rudimentary nonprison options for felons, such as plea bargaining and parole, had begun to take root. From the inside, however, the prisons were more crowded than ever. In the years between 1905 and 1909, for example, the prison population increased by 350, and there was not one new cell built in either San Quentin or Folsom. Moreover, as convict labor laws prevailed, the prisons lacked any meaningful rehabilitative programs. At Folsom, even the make-work efforts began to fail. A 1905 assembly prison committee announced that the "nearly inexhaustible" rock quarry "will soon be exhausted." Even after 1911, when a state-use law allowing convict labor to produce articles competitively for the state government passed, Folsom received no consideration for industry. Under that law San Quentin received allocations to establish "tailor shops, shoe shops, tin, machine, printing and furniture shops," but no industries were established at Folsom.[67]

Rather than the reformatory Woodworth and the California Prison Commission had wanted the Branch Prison to be, Folsom had by neglect become the institution for recidivists. A wall might have changed that. In 1917, Folsom received its official distinction as the prison for recidivists.[68] Thus, the first grading of California adult prisons was between harsh and harsher. Brutality at both prisons seemed the most effective means of control in absence of decent physical conditions and a sense of justice. For the inmates, escape was the dangerous way out of the situation. In the early twentieth century, some prisoners began to experiment with another way. Availing themselves of the reform spirit that had affected even California, these prisoners themselves became prison reformers.

CHAPTER

3

Prisoners As Reformers, 1900–1910

And some men curse, and some men weep,
And some men make no moan
From Oscar Wilde, "The Ballad of Reading Gaol"

The New Penologists and their successors, the Progressive-era penologists, had theoretical and practical suggestions as to how to rehabilitate criminals and make them functioning members of society. Their prison programs included separate one-person-per-cell prisons for juveniles, women, the criminally insane, recidivists, and, especially, first-time male offenders, some of whom could learn to become contributing members of society. In addition, their penal program provided incentives for personal achievement while in prison. These included the indeterminate sentence, which was intended to give the inmate (and, of course, the professional penologist) some control over the length of his sentence, and parole, which allowed qualified convicts to spend part of their term in the community while reporting regularly to an administering body. Finally, the penal reform program included probation, a means by which certain young or nonthreatening convicts could avoid serving a prison term altogether.

By the beginning of the twentieth century, the state of California had adopted only a few of these changes, most notably separate institutions for juveniles. Because the state was especially resistant to spending money or employing convict labor for prison construction, Progressive-era reform philosophy reflected little within the confines of San Quentin and Folsom. Rather, turn-of-the century penal practices within the overcrowded prisons strove mainly to achieve the short-term goal of trouble-free custodianship.[1] Even as other western states, such as Washington and Utah, opened adult reformatories in the first decade of the twentieth century, the California legislature refused to appropriate building funds.[2] An exception to this was an appropriation in 1903 for a separate institution for the criminally insane on the grounds of the Folsom prison.[3] Even then the expenditure proved too controversial, and in fact, it took decades for the state to build such an institution anywhere.[4] Thus it was that if California's prisons performed any rehabilitative functions at all, they did so principally by breaking the will of defiant men.

The state was not as resistant to policy changes that did not involve large expenditures of money or the use of convict labor. One important change was the creation in March 1903 of a Board of Charities and Corrections to monitor the operation of the state's various asylums.[5] Before this time, legislative committees appointed to oversee prison operations made regular visits to Folsom and San Quentin and reported back to the larger assembly. As the state government assumed more functions, however, legislators met annually rather than biennially and for longer periods of time. They simply did not have the time between lawmaking sessions to perform oversight functions as well. By the time California created its new board, nineteen other states, including some western states such as Oklahoma, had adopted similar boards. California's board functioned in tandem with the Board of Prison Directors, the latter retaining its function as a parole board and participating more directly in prison management. The six unsalaried members of the Charities and Corrections Board received a six thousand-dollar annual appropriation for expenses and a twenty-four hundred-dollar appropriation to pay the salary of a professional executive secretary. W. Almont Gates, who had previously served the state of Minnesota in the same capacity, became the new board's first secretary.[6]

In addition to creating this oversight agency in 1903, the legislature also passed the state's first probation laws. Under these laws, however, probation officers were to serve without pay, a circumstance that prevented professional administration of probation for more than a decade.[7] Although the pecuniary instincts of the state continued to rule, these laws of 1903 signaled a new receptivity to the oft-prescribed changes in the penal system.

As the prison census continued to swell, and as the frugal legislature continued to resist prison construction or improvements, Progressive-era programs that limited incarceration gained considerable repute. If more generously administered, parole would offer to prisoners the hope of escape— legally. Even the indeterminate sentence, if enacted, offered a similar promise. Some of California's Progressive-era penal reformers, therefore, were not free citizens, and some were not among the upper middle classes. Some were or had been prisoners. Rather than stage hunger strikes or riots and consequently engage the prison management in a struggle over rule enforcement, these unusual prisoners broke no written rules in the promotion of their cause. As a result, they were heard, and in itself, that victory represented a significant change in the essentially anonymous conditions of their imprisonment.

J. WESS MOORE

In California, as in numerous other states, the legislature adopted a number of means to release convicts before they had completed their full sentences. The good-time law passed in California and throughout the West as early as 1864, allowing a reduction in the total sentence, prorated for good behavior. In an 1880 modification of the original good-time law, a convict would receive a credit for two months off of his total sentence for each of his first two years of good behavior, four months off for each of the next two, and five months off for each subsequent year until his release.[8] Unlike parole, a reform designed to effect release of a prisoner professionally adjudged to be self-reliant and rehabilitated, good-time credits served as management tools. They were rewards that prison management could dispense for obedience. Exempted from the benefits of the good-time law, however, were life-sentenced convicts.

California's 1893 parole law allowed for the review of individual cases and possible early release of first-termers, except for those under a life sentence, who had served at least one calendar year in prison. Since receiving the power of parole in 1893, the Board of Prison Directors averaged twelve or thirteen paroles per year, in contrast to, say, Illinois, which then averaged one thousand per year. In 1901 the amended parole law added life-termers to the eligible list, provided they had served at least seven years.[9] Even then, the Board of Prison Directors, the functioning parole board, continued to apply the law very sparingly, in response to a furious public outcry against releasing prisoners. Among other things, the board required proof of outside employment and purchase, at the prisoner's expense, of such necessities as train tickets, even while the prisoners had no way to earn money inside. Resolutely, the board refused to hear arguments for the release of life-termers.[10] Thus, life-termers had no real hope for any amelioration in their sentences when the new century began.

J. Wess Moore, however, a San Quentin life-termer convicted of killing a claim jumper, found hope in the new spirit of reform. Within the prison he formed an organization of life-sentenced prisoners to lobby for a change in the early release laws, so that life-termers could have a chance to regain their freedom. The story of Moore, his initiative, and the various reactions to it on the outside reveal much about the social goals of imprisonment as well as the efficacy of using the system to change the system.

Life-sentenced convict number 18759, also known as J. Wess Moore, is the active protagonist of this piece. Biographical and autobiographical information on Moore from various prison census sources and from a 1909 or 1910 publication issued in his honor by the Society for the Friendless in California indicates that he was born in 1846 in a Quaker town, Dublin, Indiana. In spite of his exposure to Quaker passivism, he longed to fight for the Union cause during the Civil War. During the first year or so, he was too young to enlist as a soldier, but he joined the hostilities anyway as a drummer boy and camp follower with the Army of the Cumberland and later he marched with General Sherman to, in his words, "bloody Atlanta." [11] Both nonviolence and violence were themes of Moore's youth.

When the war was over, Moore returned to farming in Indiana. After being washed out by floods there, he and his wife moved to Nebraska, where once again he suffered the vagaries of weather—this time a cyclone destroyed his farm. Moore's next move was to California, where he staked a mining claim in Trinity County, outside of Weaverville. There he met enemies even more ominous than Mother Nature: claim jumpers and the penal laws of California. The facts of the case against Moore were never in dispute. Several times, three men had threatened Moore with violence unless he handed over his claim. At least once, Moore had reported these threats to the local district attorney, D. J. Hall, hoping to have his tormentors arrested. That never happened. When, then, early in 1900 the three once again menaced Moore and his wife, Moore fatally shot one, whose name was Alverson.[12]

The story of his crime reveals Moore as a man who apparently would first seek lawful means by which to redress what he believed to be a personal injustice. Charged with murder for killing the claim jumper, he was convicted and sentenced on September 5, 1900, to life imprisonment. At the time of sentence, a life sentence was, for all practical purposes, immutable. Therefore, when Moore entered San Quentin on October 23, 1900, a year and a half before the brutal reign of Warden John W. Tompkins commenced, he faced what he called a "living death."[13]

During his stay at San Quentin, Moore reflected angrily on the trap of life imprisonment. Even through his anger, however, he was able to know that what he really required was a legal means by which to regain his freedom:

> Surrounded by misery and woe as I am today [he wrote in his cell at San Quentin], how can I be generous in thought, deed, or act, while I see men of my own country and home,—some of whom were my comrades in the blue uniform of the United States—standing over me with rifle shotted, listening to catch my every word, noting my every move, keeping an hourly record of my life and ready to shoot me down unarmed as I am at the very first move I may make looking that I shall attempt to flee this enduring death without lawful procedure; and thus it is that I sometimes wonder "have our people fully appreciated my services to our country?"

As he wrote those words, however, he seemed discouraged about changing his desperate situation, for he concluded: "Yet, with all this I am willing to concede that the existing conditions [for me] must of necessity continue indefinitely. . . . [But] it seems hard."[14]

THE SCANDAL OF SAN QUENTIN

When Moore arrived at the California State Prison, San Quentin, it was in a disreputable condition. Because a public outcry over competition from prison labor had resulted in a state constitutional provision outlawing any prison enterprise that competed with any private enterprise in California, San Quentin had only one prison industry: a jute grain bag factory. Moore, aged fifty-four on admission, received assignment there. After fourteen back-breaking months at the jute factory, Moore, who could now walk only with the aid of two canes, received from then Warden Martin Aguirre an assignment as the prison librarian. This relatively happy condition lasted until Warden Tompkins, under whom San Quentin scandals raged, tossed Moore into an "incorrigible" cell, the term there for solitary confinement, after accusing him of smuggling tobacco. Moore, however, had already made a good impression on some of the prison directors, a group of governor-appointed laymen overseeing prison administration. One of them, James Wilkins, who was later to write a popular history of the prison, ordered Moore released from solitary confinement. Tompkins, however, had his revenge by reassigning Moore to pick jute. This Moore did for twenty months, but in the meantime, the barbarous conditions of San Quentin came to light, in part because of Tompkins's contempt not only for prisoners, but also for the prison system and the press.[15]

Early in 1903 the state assembly, having heard the California Prison Commission's reports of cruel punishments in the two state prisons, authorized the standing committee on the prisons to investigate conditions. This brief investigation uncovered such horrors that the assembly immediately assigned a select committee to undertake fuller scrutiny. Investigators were uniformly shocked. The opium traffic within San Quentin had presumably ended, but that was the only good news reported, as the select committeemen concluded that "our two prisons are no credit to the State."[16]

To start, both prisons were seriously overcrowded, as they had been consistently since each opened. In San Quentin one large room housed forty-five prisoners. Most cells held four or five. Although California legislators, prison directors, and wardens were aware of the penological theories dictating 1) classification of prisoners according to a professional assessment of the degree of their commitment to crime, and 2) segregation of like criminals so as to prevent first offenders from contact with more hardened criminals and sodomists, the select committee noted that these theories were nowhere applied: "California boasts its place in the front rank of States, but her prisons lag a generation behind the better class of Eastern penitentiaries. The two prisons are schools of vice and universities of crime." The committeemen thoroughly scolded the people of California for allowing such a situation:

The responsibility of this great wrong rests primarily not with the Wardens or yet with the Board of Prison Directors, but upon the people of California, who have followed a false idea of economy, and, steeped in neglect of public affairs, have failed to provide means for the proper conduct of these institutions. California, vaunting her wealth, ostentatious in hospitality, self-complacent, has left the beautiful shore at San Quentin, looking out on Berkeley, Oakland, and the Bay of San Francisco, to become an overgrown county jail of the old style, a jumble of buildings of all shapes and no shape, without method or design, where fifteen hundred convicts are housed at night in six hundred and forty cells, and huddled by day, when not at work, in a small yard, like a drove of cattle.[17]

At San Quentin, as at Folsom, notoriety surrounded the use of the heinous straight-jacket method of corporal punishment. The "appliance" was apparently Tompkins's preferred disciplinary device. Stories of men forever crippled after guards cinched them motionless and breathless in these canvas body vices had leaked to the press. Even though the Board of Prison Directors had abolished the use of the straight jacket at Folsom in 1902, the guards at San Quentin used it more than ever and, according to legislative committee witnesses, to a far greater extent than was officially recorded. While committee members debated the use of punishments for "insubordinate" prisoners, all called for the abolishment of the straight jacket. It was variously labeled "cruel," "un-American," "inhumane," and "debasing both to victim and the guard administering the punishment."[18]

A minority report of the select committee was even more sympathetic to the prisoners. The two who issued the minority report disagreed that the apparent docility of the inmates at San Quentin represented good discipline, but instead suggested that there existed an unhealthy compliance: "Our observations lead us to believe that the Warden has, by working on the fears of the convicts of their being killed or permanently disabled, and by use of the strait-jacket, so cowed the convicts that there is a show of confidence and respect, but it is only induced by fear." These two called for immediate dismissal of the warden, the prison physician, and the current Board of Prison Directors as a prelude to revamping the entire system to match, at least, the best standards of such institutions elsewhere in the United States. While the Board of Charities and Corrections offered a moderate voice on the subject of the straight jacket, saying, "It's present use should be limited by law and carefully regulated by the Prison Directors," the legislature had tossed the gauntlet of prison reform, and the public was to pick it up, as was Moore.[19]

THE PUBLIC DEBATE, THE PRESS, AND WARDEN TOMPKINS

J. Wess Moore, then, entered San Quentin at a critical point in the prison's history. Here was a brutal prison with no more adherence to penological dictates than a county jail. Here, too, though, was an embarrassed legislature exposing cruelty and vice and demanding reform. This legislative indignation sparked a public debate, the first ever of such length in California, over the nature of penal laws and the role of prisons. Reformers from such established groups as the California Prison Commission once again took the opportunity to promote indeterminate sentencing, classification, and segregation. Broad-based reform groups, such as the Woman's Christian Temperance Union, also lobbied for legislated reform and supported local prisoner aid societies. The Commonwealth Club, an organization of progressive San Francisco businessmen, arranged to hear speakers on various penological subjects. These civic leaders heard, to their horror, that women and still sometimes boys served their time at San Quentin rather than at separate institutions, and their voices joined in the chorus for parole reform, indeterminate sentencing, classification, and segregation. The theme of these reformers echoed that of the select committee: California's prisons had to be made to match the standards set in the East.[20]

Newspaper editors entered the debate, too. The major oppositional voices rang in the newspaper columns, for here, those "people of California" whom the committee condemned for their neglect of public affairs and their false economy defended themselves. Often, at this level, the public debate failed to penetrate a seemingly pervasive hatred for people who had committed crimes and, therefore, in some cases it did not get beyond the undisputed question of whether criminals deserved punishment to examine what punishment they did (or did not) deserve. Often, resentment of prisoners translated into blaming them for their wretched prison conditions, or, anyway, dismissing them as beasts deserving of such conditions. A December 27, 1904, editorial in the *San Francisco Post*, for example, acknowledged that state prison conditions

8. Gothic-style front entrance to San Quentin, early 1900s. (San Quentin Museum Association.)

were "unspeakable," but claimed that prisoners themselves were "more than content" with the existing foul conditions.[21]

Not all newspapers reflected such an unprogressive view of prisoners as unredeemable beasts. For example, a lively advocate of reform, the *San Francisco Examiner*, published the report of the select committee, editorialized sympathetically, and dogged Tompkins and the stories of his cruelty until Tompkins was removed as warden in 1906. Rival papers, however, were as apt to react against the *Examiner* as against prisoners. The *San Benito Advance*, for example, published an editorial on September 30, 1904, entitled, "Of Course It Is Cruel." In part, the editorial said, "The biennial rant of the Examiner about cruelty at the State prison is now on, and the hysterical shrieking of strait jacket torture is calculated to move a sphinx to tears. . . . Within the walls of San Quentin are congregated some of the greatest scoundrels on earth. . . . The head of a State prison is necessarily an autocrat, and we admire Warden Tompkins' pluck."[22]

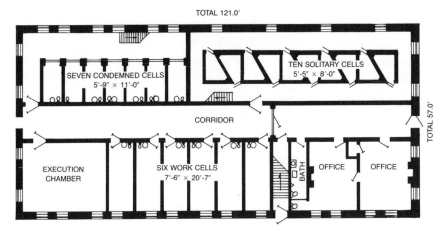

9. Plans for a new solitary building at San Quentin, to include cells for the condemned and an execution chamber, 1906. Funding for all new building was elusive in the early part of the century, and other solutions to overcrowding, such as parole, gained favor. (Redrawn by Jamie Calhoun from the original plan in the California State Archives supplied by courtesy of the Office of the Secretary of State, Sacramento.)

So went the public debate—a dialectic between sympathy and antipathy, where reformers, wanting to stay the hand of brutality, identified with and were identified with the prisoners and where conservatives, wanting to relinquish control to an authority, identified with and were identified with the warden. Ultimately, it was Tompkins's contempt, not just for the prisoners under his care, but for the prison system, the legislature, the Board of Prison Directors, and the press as well, that caused his downfall and that of the office of autocratic warden.

A brief synopsis of the public revelations about Tompkins include his 1904 defense of the straight jacket as "humane"; his repeated suggestion to eliminate the state prisons and "herd" convicts onto an island; his 1904 demand for rapid-fire artillery for use in prison defense; his 1905 cover-up of a riot in the solitary confinement, or "incorrigible," cells, which included a dismissal of guards who refused to administer the prescribed punishments; his trumped-up charge of smuggling against the prison dentist; and his claim that an obviously murdered prisoner had "committed suicide." When the Board of Prison Directors initiated an official investigation of Tompkins's management, he refused to cooperate, withholding such evidence as punishment record books. By this time even the *Examiner*'s rivals were calling for

Tompkins's removal. Early in 1906 the directors dismissed Tompkins and selected a former captain of the yard, John C. Edgar, as his immediate successor. Edgar's term was relatively short and halcyon; in 1907, John Hoyle began a ten-year stint as what came to be called San Quentin's "first modern warden." [23]

MOORE AS REFORMER

J. Wess Moore's health suffered during his years under Tompkins, as he labored in the jute mill. Also, he had lost his wife of twenty-eight years, who had found work in the home of a San Quentin guard to be near him. He claimed she died of a "broken heart." [24] Her devotion had touched him deeply. Like many inmates, Moore became a nighttime poet, and several of his creations speak to and of her. They also bespeak his literacy. But his organizing and reform activities that contributed to the penological debate of his time bespeak loudest his inherent abilities. In the midst of the Tompkins scandals, on March 27, 1904, Moore formed a "permanently organized committee" called the Life Prisoners of California Committee. Fellow committee members were M. Meyers and F. L. Wood, and the committee's goal was to seek a change in the law to permit early release of life-sentenced convicts who performed well. [25]

While the story of the formation of this committee is lost, Moore himself credited Tompkins and Captain of the Yard Harrison with making it possible. It is known, on the other hand, that Tompkins at least once had Moore punished for attempting to release a newspaper story about the life-termers plight. Possibly August Drahms, an aging but respected prison chaplain and committed reformer, provided support and literature and served as a conduit. Certainly, Drahms's introduction to a tribute volume published for Moore suggests the possibility. The first public act of the life prisoners' committee occurred in January 1905, when it issued a press release, or advertisement, calling for "clemency, justice, and mercy" and vowing to plead the cause before the whole state. Records do not reveal whether this caused retribution within the prison. Some members of the press thought that it should. The author of a January 17, 1905, editorial in the *Los Angeles Times*, entitled

"About 'Prison Reform' " was aghast at learning of the prisoners' consorting to make change, legal or otherwise:

> The astounding statement is made that the prisoners in San Quentin have a regularly organized society formed for the purpose of securing legislation in their favor. . . . It is not at all to be wondered at that convicts in the State prisons should be anxious to shorten their terms of imprisonment . . . but it seems incredible that the authorities of any prison could . . . permit the organization of a society within the prison walls for the purpose of attempting to modify the laws of the land. . . . It is retrogression.[26]

Fortunately for the life-termers, not everyone in the state felt as the *Times* editors did. Primed by two years of nearly continuous prison scandal, many applauded Moore and his committee when, in April 1905, they sent to the legislature a petition requesting a law "fixing some given number of years of good conduct and faithful service as a limit of the duration of a sentence of life imprisonment." The mechanism for applying good-time credits to a life sentence was unclear. No one really knew how long any such sentence would endure for any given convict. The newly formed Board of Charities and Corrections opposed such legislation, arguing that reduction of sentences needed to correlate with a convict's rehabilitation, as assessed professionally, rather than as a simple reward for good behavior. The board, however, sympathized with the life-termers' goal and recommended changes in the parole law to make parole truly accessible to life-termers. Other popular opinion was also more flexible than the *Times*. The *Sacramento Bee*, for example, opposed the request but not the ability of the prisoners to make the petition. The *San Jose Mercury* actually trumpeted the petition, calling it "worthy of the attention of the legislature," and used its appearance to remind readers of the need for a "system of nonpolitical, scientific penology."[27]

Moore's committee aroused some very powerful people in state government as well, including Governor George Pardee and F. C. Prescott, chairman of the newly formed California State Prison Commission. The "prison question" was starting to intrigue state officials; the state prison commission, longing to evaluate the California situation in larger terms, devised a questionnaire to send to the directors of prisons throughout the country. In it, the commission asked about mechanisms for classifying and segregating prisoners, types of employment, provisions for health care, safety, education, entertainment, visitation, religious training, and for punishment. Significantly, the commission also wanted to know how to enact an effective parole law.[28]

As it happens, the commission received very few responses to its questions. A Florida warden was even annoyed at having been asked to take time to respond. Not daunted, the commissioners and a special committee of the assembly continued their fact-finding at home; when they did, they turned to J. Wess Moore to enlighten them as to changes needed in California. Apparently, Moore carried on a detailed exchange with members of these official bodies, although only two of the letters, from Prescott's secretary to Moore, still exist. In the one, Prescott asked for arguments from Moore to refute the contention that it is "consistent with the theory of imprisonment that a man should be absolutely and irrevokably imprisoned for life." In the other, Prescott addressed a series of points apparently made in earlier correspondence with Moore. Moore must have claimed that the provision in the 1902 parole law making it possible for life-termers to apply for parole after serving seven full years actually did "more harm than good," and Prescott asked for elaboration on this point.

Although Moore's response is lost, he may have meant that isolation from society for seven full years made it nearly impossible for life-termers to meet the employment and cash prerequisites for parole. Alternatively, he may have agreed with the Board of Charities and Corrections that seven years was too short a time for the Prison Directors to sympathize with a life-termer's request for parole. Prescott further asked Moore why the Board of Prison Directors had not employed its parole power and why Moore recommended that parole reform include a parole board composed exclusively of actual prison administrators.[29]

The mandate of Prescott's committee was to recommend to the state a program for prison reform, and the committee took J. Wess Moore, a life-sentenced inmate of San Quentin, very seriously. In itself, this was a significant victory for Moore.

GRIFFITH J. GRIFFITH

Griffith J. Griffith, convicted of shooting and wounding his wife, served two years in San Quentin, from 1904 to late 1906. Before his imprisonment, he was a very successful businessman and philanthropist in Los Angeles. It was he who donated the land for Griffith Park there, and it was he who was to donate the many thousands of dollars required to buy a telescope and establish the Griffith Observatory. Born in Wales in 1852, Griffith had made his fortune in mining in California. A man who endorsed the recreation reforms of the Progressive era, Griffith donated the land for Griffith Park to the city of Los Angeles in the 1890s. Trouble began for him in 1903 when, during an argument with his wife, Griffith pulled a gun and shot her, an assault from which she recovered, but for which he was tried and convicted. Because of his prominence, his criminal trial was well-publicized, as were his divorce trial and contest for custody of his son. His ameliorated sentence came down on March 11, 1904, and he began serving his two years in San Quentin, even while his attorneys sought unsuccessfully to have the sentence overturned.[30]

The two years behind bars exposed Griffith to a side of life he had already decided to combat. Commenting on his 1890s donation of parkland to the city of Los Angeles, Griffith wrote in his unpublished autobiography, "Sunlight and air are the first requisites of sanity and health. Things that grow in the dark are unwholesome and lives lived in dark tenements are abnormal. . . . Crime and degeneracy can best be battled with a pleasure ground."[31] San Quentin was no pleasure ground under the best of circumstances, and, like Moore, Griffith arrived there during some of the institution's worst years.

Griffith was miserable in San Quentin. He was not paroled, and his attorneys even tried to get the state's supreme court to overturn his sentence, but to no avail. One surviving letter he wrote from the prison to his son on December 20, 1905, told, probably for the benefit of both the prison censors and the child, how Griffith was maintaining his equanimity even while "tying 5,000 weaver's knots daily in order to keep a twenty-spool machine busy." Even in prison Griffith saw his role as special. He wrote to his son, "I aim also in my conduct and actions to make the officers and prisoners with whom I come in contact better men." A more bitter side also showed in the letter, one that Griffith attributed to an unnamed fellow prisoner, whom he claimed to be quoting in the following passage: "Words fail to express the torture of the first awful days in San Quentin Prison; the forced wearing of striped clothes, and the many other forms of humiliation; the lonely cold cells; the remorse; the heart-hardening power of stern discipline which regulates toil and diet, waking, and sleeping." [32] San Quentin was not a park, but Griffith did not see himself as an ordinary inmate incapable of making changes.

Griffith regained his freedom in December of 1906. Two of the bills he had helped to author had already passed the assembly by the time Griffith appeared at a Board of Prison Directors meeting in mid-February 1907, hoping for a chance to speak. One of the bills mandated the long-advocated classification and segregation of state prisoners according to their degree of tractability; the other removed parole power from the Board of Prison Directors and established a Board of Pardons, Paroles, and Relief as a permanent, unpaid board charged with administering the early-release laws. Part of this latter law provided for probation officers to enforce the laws on a day-to-day basis. As a newspaper commentator noticed, "Taking away the power of paroles from the present Prison Board indicated the spot where the shoe 'pinches' some of its members." Indeed, the president of the board, Robert Devlin, adjourned the meeting as Griffith rose to speak. [33]

Although it was in March of 1907 when the legislative committee took note of the niggardly parole record of the board and suggested change, the board responded without defensiveness in its biennial report of June 30, 1907. "We have been conservative in the exercise of the [parole] power conferred upon us by law," the directors acknowledged, "but we think that we may say with pardonable pride that the results of its exercise by the Prison Board of California has demonstrated that it is highly beneficial." The pride came from the low recidivism rate of 5 percent that the board experienced by such careful use of the parole law. The directors' use of that statistic angered Griffith who said, "Why not add that if none had been paroled a still better showing could have been made?" [34]

Both of Griffith's laws passed the legislature, with the backing of reform organizations such as the Woman's Christian Temperance Union, which were beginning to affect state politics. Governor James N. Gillett, however, signed neither bill. Even so, the Board of Prison Directors hired a professional parole officer in 1908, established him in an office in San Francisco, and set about to modify the rules governing parole. On September 27, 1909, the board adopted a new set of such rules and, although they appear to be quite stringent, they also, in fact, represent reform. It was under these rules that life-sentenced convicts such as J. Wess Moore found a hearing. The impelling change was rule number 1, which required the prison wardens to maintain a "full and accurate record" of each prisoner, and thereby augment the impressionistic data that otherwise governed board decisions. In 1906 the directors had paroled just 49 men. In 1908 they paroled 197, and the number of releases continued to rise, particularly with changes in 1910 in the leadership of the board.[35]

PAROLE AND OTHER REFORMS TAKE EFFECT

A program of prison reform did follow these events in California. Although it took another three decades to build separate institutions for women offenders and for male first offenders, California undertook a massive building program at both San Quentin and Folsom so as to relieve some of the overcrowding and to try classifying and segregating prisoners. Internally, prisoners found new opportunities for vocational education, reading, and recreation. San Quentin prisoners started a newspaper in the second decade of the twentieth century. The legislature abolished corporal punishment. Reforms in the laws of prison terms occurred, too; these were designed to give professional penologists more control over the length of the prisoners' stay.

In light of parole reform, J. Wess Moore's committee lost its battle for a law foreshortening the life sentence of well behaved life-termers. More in tune with Progressive ideals, the legislature instead responded to Griffith's and Moore's quest for justice by changing the parole law. The changes allowed life-termers to become eligible for parole after eight (rather than just seven) years and established means through which life-termers could acquire the parole requirements of having employment and travel funds. This was to be accomplished through the aid of professional parole officers.[36] This was not the guarantee of release that Moore's committee had sought, but it did provide mechanisms by which parole could work.

J. Wess Moore, a man described as "looking more like Uncle Sam than anyone you know," left San Quentin on December 1, 1908, almost eight years exactly after he had entered. He thus became one of the first paroled life-termers in the state of California. To his extreme chagrin, expressed in a prison poem, he was reincarcerated on October 8, 1909, for a parole violation, the nature of which is unrecorded. Moore's story, however, does not end there. On August 20, 1910, he was reparoled to his home state of Indiana, and there he remained free.[37]

Credit for relaxation of the parole rules belonged in great part to Griffith, even though it was the 1930s before California created a separate Board of Prison Terms. He had agitated successfully for change and, through his public activities, had called attention to the resistance of the Board of Charities and Corrections in complying with the intent of the parole law. He was not as successful with his attempt to establish classification and segregation programs, for even the law that had passed through the legislature had only required such obedience to New Penology principles insofar as the current prison buildings allowed. Segregation of prisoners first occurred in 1917, when Folsom became the institution for hardened criminals, but that mostly meant further neglect of Folsom programs.

Griffith continued his pursuit of prison reform in an undaunted manner. He advocated an indeterminate-sentence law in 1907 and beseeched Californians to update their penal system. Many reform groups echoed his sentiments toward the indeterminate sentence, but no such law passed for another ten years.[38] He was a frequent figure at speaking engagements and in the newspapers. He even formed a group called the Prison Reform League in April 1909.

In 1910, Griffith asserted that there were four thousand California members of the Prison Reform League and called the league's greatest function the "creation of an indignant public opinion." He issued weekly bulletins to California newspapers. Griffith was the league's secretary and treasurer and "principal organizer." It is not clear whether there were other officers or whether the creation of the league was Griffith's ingenious way of continuing to be heard without seeming to be a voice in the wilderness. Certainly, the most enduring product of the Prison Reform League was the 1910 publication, in book form, of *Crimes and Criminals*.[39] In this three hundred-page volume, the book's authors detail gruesome prison stories. Included is a chapter explicitly by Griffith, entitled "San Quentin As I Knew It," where he detailed the ineptitude of prison officials, the straight jacket and other tortures, the murder of inmates, and the daily monotony that alternately angered and enervated the men.

In grand fashion, Griffith dedicated *Crimes and Criminals* to Leo Tolstoy, sent the dying master a copy, and used the occasion of Tolstoy's acknowledgment as a news story to announce publication of the book. The *Los Angeles*

Herald, for example, published the story on December 31, 1910, with the headline, "Angeleno Prizes Tolstoy's Letter: Probably Last of Sage's Communications Was Received by Griffith J. Griffith." The body of the article, however, reprinted the comparatively lengthy letter Griffith sent to Tolstoy explaining the reform mission of the book; Tolstoy's return letter merely thanked Griffith and indicated the great author would certainly read it at some time in the future.[40]

Griffith's prison reform activities apparently slowed after publication of *Crimes and Criminals*. Perhaps Griffith was satisfied with the directions California was taking under Governor Pardee, with its newly constituted prison board and parole officers in place, and the removal of the heavy-handed wardens. Because *Crimes and Criminals* contained an exposé of the exceptionally squalid conditions in San Quentin's women's quarters, the book very successfully gained sympathy for prison reform among the state's clubwomen. Perhaps the growing activities of the clubwomen satisfied his desire to keep prison issues alive. Certainly he did not fade entirely from the public eye. In 1912, for example, Griffith, with his wonted fanfare, donated an observatory to the city of Los Angeles.[41]

During the four years of his reform activity, Griffith, in his flamboyance, succeeded in his goal of creating public indignation about prison conditions. Inmates wrote letters to the newspapers thanking Griffith for his efforts, clubwomen such as Hester Griffith (no relation) of the WCTU attributed much growing public support to his work, legislators introduced his bills, and journalists published his speeches and stories.[42] Unlike J. Wess Moore, Griffith J. Griffith did not owe his freedom to his own efforts, nor was he otherwise without wealth and influence. But like Moore, Griffith was a strong believer in his right to be heard, even if he was a convict and even, or maybe especially, if the Board of Prison Directors shunned him. These stories of J. Wess Moore and Griffith J. Griffith illustrate how their craving for personal liberty helped others to focus on the appropriateness or inappropriateness of long-term incarceration and of corporal punishment in a democratic society, which Progressive-era California was increasingly, if painfully, becoming. The extent to which a society is democratic, that is, the extent to which it prizes personal liberty and accepts individual differences, is the extent to which deprivation of liberty alone, without the additional humiliation of straight jackets or solitary confinement, is severe punishment. As Moore and Griffith both saw it, a modern penal system required that the individual have as much dignity as possible while incarcerated and have the hope of reshaping his future through such means as parole or the indeterminate sentence. In the case of Moore, especially, a man whose self-definition included the ability to take personal action, an immutable life sentence was, arguably, a cruel punishment. Nevertheless, he gained hope from the reforms of the era and tried to change his immutable fate rather than submit or escape illegally. Moore gained a hearing in the 1900s, in part through the formation of a unified committee voice. Griffith also made himself heard, and he also used a reform organization to amplify his message. Such hearings were unprecedented in California and, in themselves, they denoted a society evolving toward a more complete democracy, and one in which reform groups touting segregated prisons for women and first offenders might have influence.

CHAPTER

4

Minimum Security for the Fallen Women,

1910–1936

With mop and mow, we saw them go,
Slim shadows hand in hand
From Oscar Wilde, "The Ballad of Reading Gaol"

Female prisoners in California were the first of the state convicts to achieve a separate minimum security prison. From the beginning, state legislators anticipated that there would be female convicts; the 1851 legislation establishing a state prison mandated that female prisoners would have a separate building from male prisoners and that they would also labor and eat separately.[1] The purpose of this segregation was mainly to avoid sexual contact between the male and female prisoners rather than to establish a distinct rehabilitation program for the women. In fact, the state and San Quentin managed to ignore both the 1851 provision for a separate building and the female felons as well until a Progressive-era exposé of their squalid conditions led to reformers demanding change from reluctant prison administrators. The reformers' interest in the women, the hesitation of male prison administrators to create programs for women with such limited economic and domestic potential, and the growing numbers of woman convicts, in turn, led eventually to a separate California Institution for Women near Tehachapi in Kern County. In 1933, the Institution for Women opened to receive all of the female prisoners from San Quentin, regardless of whether their crime was murder, check forgery, or prostitution, whether they were first-termers or recidivists, and whether their sentence was for one year or for life, as long as it was less than death. In effect, therefore, woman criminals became a criminal classification of their own, and, by authorizing a separate facility for them, the legislature finally built a minimum security prison.

WOMEN IN STATE PRISONS IN THE

NINETEENTH CENTURY

The plans architect Ferdinand Vassault submitted in 1852 for the State Prison at San Quentin called for nine cells for women, each with its own window, in a building separate from the men.[2] Controversy over the proposed expenditures for the prison immediately ensued, and Vassault's plans were never realized. The few female convicts (there were up to five of them at a time during the 1850s) who were sentenced to the state prison became part of the scandal of Estell's administration.[3] Although the women had quarters separate from the men, first in the cabin of the prison brig and then in the overseer's house, their activities were not kept separate. Some of the 1855 testimony contained in the report of the Grand Jury of Marin County, investigating corruption at the state prison, indicated that a guard named John Gray regularly slept with a female prisoner, Dolores Martinez, and that a guard captain named Thompson was known to have sexual intercourse with a convict named Mary Ann Wilson, or "Scotch Mary."[4]

Concern over this wantonness at the state prison seemed to focus at least as much on the general laxity of discipline as on the well-being of the female convicts. Certain legislators thought the best way to deal with the women was to keep them out of the state prison, regardless of their crime. To this end, the joint committee investigating affairs at San Quentin in 1858 recommended removing all women as well as all male convicts with a sentence of less than two years from the prison. It was the committee's idea that the women and the first offenders could serve their sentences in the county of their conviction, where they could "do public works." Nonetheless, the state, once it returned the prison to the lessees, insisted that providing for a separate women's building was a condition of the lease. In 1857, the state's Board of Prison Com-

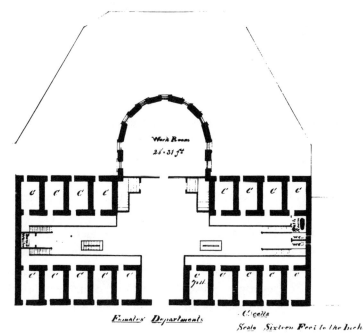

10. 1857 plan for the "Females' Department" of San Quentin. A bathroom and two water closets lay at one end of the corridor separating the cells, and a dumb waiter lay at the other. This room remained the women's quarters until the new women's building opened in the 1920s. (California State Archives, Office of the Secretary of State, Sacramento; photograph by Everett Weinreb.)

missioners hired architect Miner F. Butler to design a building for use as a hospital, dining room, and female department and ordered the lessee, Estell, to begin the work. According to Butler, Estell agreed to begin, but, because of an unexplained dispute between him and the sublessee, McCauley, no one ever procured the building materials or permitted Butler to begin the work in any other way. McCauley apparently had no intention of proceeding with the construction; one of his complaints filed against the state in the second contract nullification case was that it had illegally ordered the lessees to construct this fifty to eighty thousand-dollar building.[5]

By the time the state resumed control over the prison for the second time in 1858 and began constructing new prison buildings, the female population had declined to two, and, by 1860, to zero. Although the male prisoner population increased steadily for the next twenty years, the female population remained under ten until 1879, a year when the total San Quentin population was 1,554. In 1880, Folsom Prison began receiving inmates, including one woman who arrived there in 1885.[6] Total numbers of female prisoners first hit twenty in 1885, and the following year they were twenty-nine out of a total of 1,891. This increase did not represent a trend, however, because during the next thirteen years, until 1900, the median female prisoner population was sixteen, while the median male population was 2,032; women were well under 1 percent of the total prisoner population.

As such a small and bewildering minority of an already detested minority group—convicts—female prisoners received virtually no attention during most of the nineteenth century. Even some of the most seemingly detailed biennial reports of the prison directors, wardens, turnkeys, physicians, and moral instructors failed to mention the female prisoners, even in passing.[7] Overcrowding and convict-labor issues dominated the administrative reports and the concerns of the visiting legislators as well. An 1897 inventory of buildings at San Quentin mentions "one building, containing the offices of the Captain of the Yard and Turnkey, clothing room, barber shops, etc., on the lower floor, and the female prison on the upper floor," and this is the best description of the women's quarters contained in these official prison reports.[8]

From the institutional inattention to women, it is not even possible to know when San Quentin first hired a matron to govern and protect the female prisoners. One historian placed the date at 1875 and noted that "it was not until a prison matron was appointed that the recurrent scandals ceased about the women prisoners." Nevertheless, the 1877–79 biennial report of the prison directors lists the salaries of the officers, guards, and employees of San Quentin, but does not list a matron. Possibly "guard" subsumes the category, but it is not clear. The women also lacked any particular vocal advocate outside of the prisons, although James Woodworth of the California Prison Commission regularly inserted in his reports a case study of a reformed female criminal or a plea for a separate reformatory for criminal women. He was California's most vocal expositor of the New Penology, espoused by Enoch Wines and Theodore Dwight in 1867 and secured in the "Declaration of Principles" in 1870. Even as promoters of separate institutions for women, these most famous prison reformers offered no program of reformation for the female inmates. Instead, they defended their idea on four grounds: 1) on the moral grounds of preventing intercourse of all sorts between male and female inmates; 2) on the sanitary grounds of avoiding interior dividers in already inadequately lighted and ventilated buildings; 3) on the economic grounds that women need less costly buildings to retain them adequately, and that female keepers "would require less pay"; and 4) on the administrative grounds that separate institutions would give both the matron and the warden a distinct domain and prevent their jealously guarding their power.[9] Like his mentors, Woodworth focused most of his reform energies on the white male inmates.

Once in a while, a newspaper reporter discovered the female prisoners, usually during a visit to the greater prison. In 1867 a journalist from the *Daily Alta California* visited San Quentin and, among other things, reported on the conditions of the three women there at the time of his visit. According to this account, they were confined away from the men and left their quarters only on Sundays, when the men were partaking of the sabbath services. The women reportedly ate better than their male counterparts, because they received their food from the officers' mess. Otherwise the women were idle and had not even a matron to guide their activities. In 1888, another journalist, this one a woman from the *San Francisco Examiner*, reported on her impressions of the nearly twenty female prisoners she visited during a trip to San Quentin. She openly reacted to their idleness and their long sentences, concluding that they would be completely unequipped to make an honest living when they eventually did leave the prison walls.[10]

The neglect of California's female prisoners in the nineteenth century accorded with the treatment of female prisoners elsewhere in this country. Many western states in particular built no facilities for women at all in the nineteenth century, or even through most of the twentieth century, presumably because the low number of female convicts did not justify building quarters for them. As late as the early 1970s, Idaho still contracted with Oregon for confinement of its female convicts, Hawaii with California, and Montana, North Dakota, South Dakota, and Wyoming all contracted with Nebraska. Neglect of women prisoners was even characteristic of nineteenth-century New York and Massachusetts, where the percentage of female convicts was much greater than in California—as high as twenty percent—and where penal practice was more apt to reflect penal theory, at least regarding the male prisoners. The neglect of the women there also meant no attempt to employ the silent system or to build the cells necessary to insure isolation and privacy at night. Fallen women, as even the Reverend Woodworth called female convicts, met no one's idea of a worthy cause because, in a society that defined women as moral paragons, they were no longer fit as wives and mothers. As long as upright women shunned them and men provided no alternate economic definition, then there was nothing for the fallen women to become in any realm of the larger society.[11]

Ironically, of course, many of the women incarcerated were married and had received their sentences as accomplices to their husbands. This meant a double failure for the women, who not only had committed the crime for which they served sentences, but who had also failed their charge as moral arbiters for their husbands.[12]

The neglect the women suffered at San Quentin was real, as the absence of administrative comment throughout the nineteenth century demonstrates. The neglect was, however, in no way benign, as reforming clubwomen at the turn of the century were to discover.

THE EXPOSÉ OF THE WOMEN'S DEPARTMENT AT SAN QUENTIN

The 1870 National Prison Congress, seeking new ways to promote reformation of prisoners, recommended as its thirty-seventh principle that "the agency of woman may be employed with excellent effect." James Woodworth repeated that recommendation in his report that year. Women, nonetheless, did not appear in any decision-making capacity regarding California's prisons throughout the nineteenth century or well into the twentieth, even though the 1903 act establishing a state Board of Charities and Corrections to oversee all state institutions explicitly stated that women could hold board positions. Even without official positions, however, California clubwomen began employing their moral agency to promote a reformed society, including reformed prisons. The Woman's Christian Temperance Union of Southern California organized in 1884, and in 1885 P. J. Dimmick, the superintendent of the club's prison and police stations department, issued a report in which she announced, "Prison management in any enlightened state is no longer a matter of bolts, bars and stone walls, but is a system which requires the highest culture of head and heart." During this same time that women were beginning to join clubs and assert their reforming spirit, the conditions at San Quentin for male and female prisoners were in increasing need of reform. The squalor at San Quentin reached its nadir during the tenure of

Warden J. W. Tompkins, whose brutal regime ended in scandal and resignation in 1906. That same year, Griffith J. Griffith left San Quentin and
soon produced a horrifying account of the women's quarters there.[13] Once
the clubwomen investigated and found the unbelievable stories to be true,
they acted, first to ameliorate conditions at San Quentin, and then to build a
separate institution for women.

The published description of the women's quarters depicted a "bear pit"
sixty by ninety feet, with a cell building forty by twenty feet taking up the
middle of the space. All of the women's activities took place in the cemented
perimeter of this space, even though during the 1900s there were at least
twenty-one women prisoners at a given time and as many as thirty-one.[14] The
women were never allowed out for exercise or air, lest they communicate with
the men. For the same reason, the windows that might have let sunlight into
the space had long since been painted gray.[15]

Griffith J. Griffith's unnamed informant reported that the conditions
within this space were foul. A "hopper" in the room received all the contents
of the slop buckets, rats ran unabated at night, and no heat source warmed
the cold winter evenings. The description successfully evoked sympathy and
provoked action from the charitable clubwomen to whom it really was addressed. One paragraph discussed a woman confined twenty-three years and
intoned, "Why do not these club women, and others, try to do something for
the women, even if they are accused of murder, when men who are guilty of
the same crime are being paroled and assisted by women every month?"[16]

Hester Griffith of the WCTU was one who heeded Griffith J. Griffith's challenge to clubwomen. At least part of her response appeared at the end of his
published essay. She stated that she had corroborated the foul conditions and
she underscored the allegation that in 1904 and 1905 visiting members of the
state legislature had used the women's quarters as a brothel.[17]

There is little reason to doubt that the kinds of allegations that Griffith J.
Griffith made were true. While few of these allegations received explicit
official attention, Warden Tompkins, in his last report before his dismissal,
admitted, "The female ward is crowded and devoid of the conveniences
it should have."[18] That sentence was the entirety of his report about the
female ward.

Griffith's exposé served an especially important journalistic function for
the women. The Tompkins scandal of cruelty and mismanagement resulted
in much publicity about conditions for men at San Quentin. Straight-jacket

punishment, opium use, a network of prisoner spies, and tobacco trafficking were among the revelations in the press that shocked the public. Although conditions for the female inmates at San Quentin were horrible, the scandalized press did not pick up on the female side of the story. Out of twenty-six clippings from San Francisco newspapers dating from November 1905 to July 1906 that revealed conditions at San Quentin and called for prison reform, none addressed the problems of the women's ward.[19]

The clubwomen who responded to Griffith's call to help women prisoners worked side by side with his Prison Reform League and each other to effect reform. When Griffith presented his reform bills to the legislature in 1909, clubwomen were among his most vocal supporters. Hester Griffith, in fact, received special mention from her WCTU sisters for doing "very efficient work for these bills." Although the two Griffiths bore no relation to each other, they did have common goals of prison reform based, at least in part, on the belief that criminals were redeemable and that society was greatly to blame in their downfall. This belief in environmental determinism spurred many Progressive-era reformers, because the philosophy freed individuals from total responsibility for their own actions, on the one hand, and depicted them as inherently true to their nature, on the other. Environmental determinism, when coupled with a continuing belief in the moral superiority of women, meant a new conception of the fallen woman. No longer the temptress, like Eve, she was now the victim. It is no accident that the WCTU, in California and elsewhere, grabbed the banner for female prisoners, just as it sought to impose a certain kind of morality on men, women's chief victimizers.[20] These same clubwomen and their successors were soon to seek a separate reformatory for women in California, run by women without any male intervention. Until 1935, when they acquired enough political clout to get a constitutional amendment passed, they were to find their efforts frustrated, co-opted, or trivialized, as the needs of men, even male prisoners, were to prevail.

SONOMA: THE FIRST SEPARATE INSTITUTION

Certainly, conditions did improve for the women at San Quentin after the Prison Reform League's publication and the WCTU's endorsement of it. The reputedly cruel matron was fired and, by 1913, the Board of Prison Directors reported that "the building containing the women's ward has been completely overhauled and renovated, and several minor improvements added that tend to make it more cheerful, comfortable, and sanitary."[21] Conditions there may have remained "improved" for quite some time, in spite of a national agitation for separate women's prisons, had not World War I provided a male-oriented reason to build such an institution, and thereby set an important precedent.

Despite the National Prison Congress's strong support for such separate institutions as early as 1870, only a few states had heeded the message by the turn of the century: Indiana, Massachusetts, and New York.[22] By 1910, however, three more eastern states had actively begun to seek support for women's reformatories, and the idea began to receive increasing publicity. One important essay, in fact, alleged that men were impeding the development of separate women's prisons in order to keep the inmate women available as "jail drudges." This essay described the existing women's reformatories and explained the philosophy behind providing a farm setting rather than a dreaded mass of stone and bars. These pastoral prisons were supposed to accommodate the domesticity attributed to women's natures. Farms or farmlike settings, it was thought, provided a healthy environment in nature, and farming provided practice in nurture as well as productive work experience. Classification of the women into criminal categories was possible in a floor plan that provided each woman with her own room—not cell—with windows. Rehabilitation occurred through a program of schooling and training in marketable female skills, such as sewing, mothering, and nursing. The ideal women's reformatory had female attendants, managers, and trustees, since men could not be trusted either to understand and provide for women's needs or to avoid exploiting the women.[23] California's first attempt to build such an institution occurred in 1919, as an outgrowth of a rise in prostitution and venereal disease during the Great War.

In response to a 1916–18 report of the Board of Charities and Corrections, the state legislature passed a bill in April 1919 to establish the California Industrial Farm for Women. The report stated that the need for this institution had been "forcibly shown in the last two years of the war when prostitutes ha[d] been temporarily detained in the counties, released and floated on to the next community with no attempt of any kind for their social, mental, and physical rehabilitation." The Assembly *Journal* indicated that the bill had received petitions of support from a variety of women's clubs: the Ebell Club of Fillmore, the Poinsettia Club of Saticoy, the San Diego Women's Club, and the Tuesday Club of Ventura.[24] The Women's Legislative Council of California was a lobbying consortium representing "over seventy thousand clubwomen" in such clubs throughout the State; Hester Griffith was an overseer of the council, which initiated the bill and promoted it heavily.

A WCTU monthly newspaper, the *Southern California White Ribbon*, carried prominent stories about the bill in early 1919. Most of the articles represented the legislation's purpose as protecting the delinquent women. According to one such article, written by Hester Griffith and appearing on the front page of the March 1919 issue, the bill was designed "to provide custody, care, protection, industrial, and other training and rehabilitation for the delinquent women."[25] Indeed, those words came from Section 2 of the act itself.

Other sources, however, suggest that men saw the bill's purpose as much different, and the bill, of course, required men's backing in order to pass. Testifying before the Senate Committee on Prisons and Reformatories on behalf of the bill was the "United States Government (as) represented by Major Stanley Coor," for example. Coor told the committee that the government's interest was "more far-reaching than the mere protection of enlisted men," sounding as if that were its commonly supposed purpose. He continued, saying that since the bill provided for "the detention and examination of fallen women and their confinement to the proposed State institution, its purpose is to reduce or erase disease."[26]

Certainly, whether he purported the bill's purpose as protecting enlisted men from venereal disease or the loftier goal of eliminating venereal disease completely, the major presented a far different reason for confining the delinquent women than the clubwomen did. The major did not address the training and rehabilitation of the women at all, but only what their confinement could do to protect the men who partook of "fallen women."

Not everyone who heard the major's argument allowed it to pass unchallenged, although the mainstream women's club representatives did. A Mrs. C. E. Grosjean of San Francisco, representing an organization called the Parent's Rights League of America, was one vocal critic of the bill who denounced the double standard inherent in it. She decried incarcerating women to protect men and demanded, at the very least, that infected men be incarcerated as well. Nevertheless, the women of the Legislative Council, if they did not embrace the major's arguments or even pay attention to them, certainly did welcome his support, and the Grosjean argument did not reappear in the popular press or in the *White Ribbon*. The *San Francisco Chronicle*, in fact, announced in April 1919 that the bill had the support of "every women's club in the State." The *White Ribbon* never even acknowledged the enlisted men and venereal disease argument of the bill's male supporters. In May a lengthy article appeared in it in which Dr. Ethel Watters, of the state's Bureau of Social Hygiene, expounded a thorough program for the rehabilitation of prostitutes.[27] Perhaps the clubwomen thought that once they had achieved the industrial farm, they could operate it without further hindrance from the men. Nothing could have been further from the truth. Once the war was over, so were the concern and the appropriations.

THE SHORT LIFE OF THE SONOMA INDUSTRIAL FARM

The State Industrial Farm for Women at Sonoma resulted from the original 1919 appropriation of $150,000 to acquire a "suitable site of not less than two hundred acres with the necessary appurtenances." Although the statute called for the speedy purchase of such a site as would "afford ample opportunity for agricultural work and training for those committed to the institution," the doors of the short-lived reformatory for delinquent women did not open until January 1922, and it was situated on poor farmland. There were 645 total acres, but no more than 30 acres of them were arable.[28] The war, of course, was over by 1922, the time when Sonoma Farm received its first inmates, mostly from county jails, although San Quentin was allowed to send those committed for vice crimes. In March 1923 the main building, a forty-room residence purchased as part of the property, burned irreparably, and, rather than appropriate money to restore the institution, the legislature effectively abolished it.

Even before the fire, the legislature's proposed $45,000 appropriation over two year's time threatened the institution with "slow starvation," in the words of spokeswoman Blanche Morse. Clubwomen supported an appropriation of $230,000, mostly for buildings and other capital improvements. On March 1, 1923, just days before the main building burned, Morse, representing the San Francisco Center of the California Civic League, a women's club, spoke to the Commonwealth Club, a men's club in favor of the appropriations. She had ten minutes to present the case. In that time, she described the institution as housing sixty-five wards, although it had room for eighty, and as providing a necessary antidote to the evils of society. Morse exhorted the men to act not only to eliminate venereal disease, but also to accept society's responsibility for creating prostitutes and other fallen women. They could do the latter, she told them, by supporting an institution of rehabilitation, and she illustrated her argument with the story of the recovery of a thirty-year-old female drug addict.[29]

Rather than death by slow starvation, the Sonoma experiment died by fire. The institution closed its doors on June 30, 1923, having paroled and discharged the remaining inmates. The significance of Sonoma lay not in its success or even its promise, because it never was intended to replace the women's ward at San Quentin and so was inherently limited in its ability to serve convicted women. Rather, the significance lay in the precedence of supporting a separate reformatory for women, with a board of trustees dominated by women, and with women hired as "all regularly employed assistants, officers and employees."[30] Moreover, the legislation itself served as a model for a bill that passed a decade later, and exposure to the world of political exigencies may have helped clubwomen anticipate some of the double standards of legislation and appropriation they would encounter with the next attempt to establish a separate institution. Finally, Sonoma served as a model to such people as male prison administrators and members of the State Board of Prison Directors who longed to be rid of the female population at San Quentin.

THE NEW WOMEN'S BUILDING AT SAN QUENTIN

Conditions had markedly improved for the female inmates of San Quentin, even before their separate new building became a reality in 1927. Largely through the efforts of Hester Griffith and the WCTU, the "wholly unfit" matron of fourteen years had lost her job, to be replaced in 1916 by Josephine Jackson. As the new women's superintendent, Jackson was, by all reports, kind and even beloved. One inmate author, for example, P. Evelyn Rosencrantz, wrote a poem to Jackson on the occasion of the matron's annual vacation; the poet looked forward to Jackson's return, calling her the "brave champion of our fight," and the female prisoners her "homesick children." Another of the female inmates wrote an essay for the prison newspaper, the *Bulletin*, in which she described Jackson as "a tall, quiet woman who moves with dignity and poise, yet whose kindly, beaming face . . . has seen many scenes: comic, absurd, horrible, and tragic and yet remains unruffled through it all."[31]

Jackson's presence may have eased conditions considerably, but as long as the women had only quarters designed for nineteen inmates fifty-some years earlier, overcrowding and associated problems dominated the women's ward. The State Board of Charities and Corrections, in its report of 1918–20, had addressed the women's conditions at San Quentin more directly than ever before: the quarters were overcrowded and lacking proper ventilation and opportunity for recreation and employment. The thirty to thirty-five female inmates occasionally took walks in the countryside with Jackson, and inside they occupied themselves with work on basketry and needlepoint. Sometimes they served the male prisoners their food. But, the report concluded, "The whole problem with prison care would be simplified by removing the women prisoners from San Quentin."[32]

The overcrowding of the women's quarters was soon to become untenable, as the end of the war brought a sudden, dramatic increase in the inmate population. The women's numbers rose from thirty-four to forty in the year between 1921 and 1922, and to fifty-one in 1923.[33] The demise of the Sonoma farm and the official recognition of the crisis in the San Quentin women's ward meant that interested clubwomen turned their attention back to San Quentin and, by 1925, they successfully achieved an appropriation for a new separate women's building there. An article for the *Stockton Independent* of September 26, 1925, reprinted in the San Quentin prison newspaper, announced that 150 "representative clubwomen from all sections of the state were present at the ceremonies of breaking ground for the new building that is to be erected for the women prisoners of San Quentin." George A. Van Smith, president of the Board of Prison Directors and principal speaker at the groundbreaking, credited the clubwomen with making the building a reality and identified it with "a new epoch in the humanitarian history of California."[34]

The new three-story building, costing over four hundred thousand dollars to build and furnish, could house 120 prisoners and was outside the main prison wall, completely separate from the men's facilities. The ground floor housed the matrons' and supervisor's rooms and such public and congregate rooms as visitor reception areas and a dining hall. The second and third floors contained forty-five single rooms each, complete with a washbasin and toilet facilities, and both of those floors also contained a clinic, a laboratory, and physician and nurse facilities.[35]

The building was completed in late 1927, and the women moved in shortly thereafter. A January 1931 article published in the *Bulletin* described work in the new women's department as it had developed under Jackson's leadership and with the approval of Warden James Holohan. No longer without industry, the women, who numbered 127 by then, engaged in the making of flags for use at government offices throughout the state. Through this application of the feminine activity of sewing, the women were supposed to achieve a sense of pride both in their accomplishment and in their country. The new women's building boasted a fully equipped laundry, employing forty of the female inmates as they prepared clean linens for themselves and for some parts of the men's prison complex. Other activities were traditionally feminine ones as well: housekeeping and food preserving. Together, these meant that the women's building was "an outstanding model of domestic efficiency," where, using their skills in canning fruit, the women combated "against the rigors and monotony of prison fare," and that the women's ward was increasingly self-sustaining. The article referred to the entire women's department as a "household," for that surely was the ideal, and quoted Jackson as saying that the department was "busy minding its own business." [36]

In addition to participating in the work of maintaining this household, the women of the new department were offered in-house instruction in the few avenues of potential female employment: practical nursing, beauty culture, interior decoration, drama, sewing, toymaking, and typing and stenography. As Roberta Hall, an inmate and frequent contributor to the *Bulletin*, pointed out in a 1932 article, the state appropriated no funds for teachers for women. The courses the women's department offered, under the guidance of Jackson, depended on there being qualified instructors among the prisoners themselves. At the time of Hall's writing, a registered nurse who also staffed the hospital taught the nursing course, a beautician the cosmetology course, a certified teacher the spelling and arithmetic courses, and a secretary the typing and stenography—inmates all. Hall noted that neither the teachers nor the students received any compensation for their efforts at all, not in the form of money or good-time credits. Nonetheless, as another inmate author observed, the educational work contributed to a "new atmosphere in the department. It has stimulated beneficial conversation and discussion, and opened new vistas and horizons of hope for women." [37] In addition to Jackson's help, the new, commodious building made many of these programmatic improvements possible.

The female prisoners were not to partake of these new quarters for long, however. The clubwomen of the state were not satisfied with a women's prison run by men. Before the new quarters were even complete, Eleanor Miller, state assemblywoman and reform advocate, had introduced, "an Act to authorize the Governor to appoint a commission to prepare the plans and to select a site for a permanent penal institution for women offenders"; this act passed, and the commission began its search.[38]

Once again, the support of men was necessary to launch a project for a separate institution for women and, once again, that support rested on a male-oriented, not female-oriented, purpose. By moving the women out of their new women's building at San Quentin, the male prison administrators saw the possibility of gaining a long-awaited hospital building for the men, while finally disposing of the intractable problem of female prisoners. In fact, it seems quite likely that the male administrators wanted to retain the female prisoners just long enough to get a new building and then, as quickly as possible, transport the women elsewhere. The case for this argument is strong. Leo Stanley, San Quentin's doctor, had declared the prison's hospital facilities inadequate when he arrived in 1913. The new women's building was designed with hospital facilities on the two floors where there were living quarters. Ostensibly these treatment facilities were for the care of the women, but the design and the outfitting of the building certainly made it easy to convert it entirely to a hospital.[39]

In his memoirs, Stanley admitted, "We (he and Warden Holohan) agitated to move the women out of San Quentin. Separated as they were from the men . . . they were still a disturbing factor [with their] feuds, tears, hair-pullings, love-affairs, and letter-smuggling." Besides that, he continued, the prison hospital facilities were overcrowded and a new hospital very expensive. "The new women's building would make an ideal hospital," he declared. When the women did move out in 1933, just six years after moving in, the *Bulletin* quoted Dr. Stanley as saying he could now have, "The best prison hospital in the world."[40]

The improvements at San Quentin were real, but they did not necessarily reflect, at bottom, a change in the old pattern of male neglect of female prisoners—a fact that initially eluded the reforming clubwomen. They had achieved a separate reformatory for delinquent women only with the support of men who had the power to make it happen. Male support came for male-oriented reasons; the Sonoma farm was a way to protect a double standard of morality and enlisted men from venereal disease. When these reasons vanished, continued male support was not forthcoming, and the institution closed. Ironically, the clubwomen provided the legislature with a morally upright excuse for spending money on prison improvements ultimately intended to benefit male prisoners. Otherwise, prison appropriations often yielded criticism for the lawmakers from a vindictive public.

With San Quentin conditions for female prisoners unarguably abominable and with white, middle-class clubwomen publicly embracing the cause of their fallen sisters, male prison administrators and interested legislators found it politically easier to appropriate funds for a new women's building than for a new hospital for the men. Of course, it would also be necessary to remove the women from San Quentin before claiming the new building, but the desire of the warden, the oversight boards, the prison doctor, and the clubwomen to do that was no secret. A commission to select a site for a separate and permanent women's prison was at least in part the next step in gaining a hospital for the men of San Quentin.

CREATING THE CALIFORNIA INSTITUTION
FOR WOMEN AT TEHACHAPI

In 1929, using virtually the identical language it had used ten years earlier to establish the first reformatory for delinquent women—except that it now included female felons—the legislature passed "an Act to establish an institution for the confinement, care, and reformation of women misdemeanants and women convicted of a felony the punishment for which is less than death, to provide for its maintenance, conduct, and government." Assemblywoman Eleanor Miller, the only female state legislator at the time, had introduced the bill, just as she had introduced the earlier act appointing a commission to study plans and sites for such an institution. Miller, an English teacher, writer, and bible student, had been the choice of the local Republican party in Pasadena, just after the passage of the nineteenth amendment. Her personal interests were a cross between the moralistic ones of the pre-suffrage clubwomen and those of the post-suffrage League of Women Voters, with its wider scope. Miller embraced temperance, citizen education, and legislative protection for the special interests of women and children, and she sought to address crime problems, prisons, and reformatories. In philosophy and in deed, she represented an extension of the role of women as the model of morality within the home, but her arena for two decades was the legislature and her interest public policy. Her solution to the problem of crime helps to demonstrate this blend: "Old-fashioned religious and moral teaching, coupled with obedience to home-rule and strict temperance principles would be the best solution of our crime problems."[41] She believed that women, inherently good, even if wayward, were especially receptive to such teachings. Therefore, on the recommendation of the 1927 committee, she rewrote the 1919 legislation, and in 1929 the state authorized $475,000 to be spent establishing the new women's reformatory.

Passage of the act was the easy part. As authorized, the Board of Trustees comprised three women and two men: Rose Wallace as chair, Emily D. Latham, Gertrude Slocum, Fred D. Parr, and J. Frank Burke. The board's first task was to locate and purchase a suitable site, of at least fifty acres, capable of supporting inmate agricultural work. After an eight-month search, the board purchased a 1,683-acre site in the Cummings Valley of the Tehachapi Mountains in Kern County, eleven miles from the town of Tehachapi, for $110,000. The chairman of the Board of Trustees, Rose Wallace, announced the purchase with pride: "The board believes the site ideal for a corrective institution." She went on to explain that the weather was never too hot and, even in the winter, "the frosty, bracing weather . . . will not only provide variety in necessarily monotonous lives, but will work with us in our endeavor to have these unfortunate women learn the joys of useful labor." Moreover, the site had an abundance of good water, from springs and wells, and had met with approval of an array of state experts: the state architect, state water engineers and soil experts, and state medical authorities.[42]

The site selection, nonetheless, became a subject of controversy, as Wallace asserted, in the "heat of the campaign last year." The claim that the property was a desert wasteland, where nothing would grow because of poor soil, climate, and inadequate water threatened further expenditures for facilities to make the proposed institution operable. The claim was serious enough to suspend progress while a senate-authorized special committee investigated "the desirability of the site." In May of 1931 that committee, accompanied by the engineer of the State Department of Public Works, the superintendent of the Napa State Farm and supervisor of Agriculture for the Department of Institutions, and an engineer from the Division of Water Rights made an exploratory site visit. While recommending that the proposed location of the building complex be moved to higher and more fertile ground, the special committee strongly endorsed the overall purchase and vindicated the board, concluding "that no better site could be selected in the State."[43]

On recommendation of the committee, therefore, the state released the funds set aside to start construction. The Board of Trustees felt triumphant, as shown in a letter Rose Wallace wrote to the *Sausalito News*, inviting others to visit the new institution site. However, the quickly resolved site controversy did not end the frustrations the board faced in getting the new, separate reformatory up and running, although the resolution to this initial problem did allow groundbreaking to occur. Nine months after the originally scheduled groundbreaking, on June 18, 1931, Josephine Jackson, superintendent of the women's department at San Quentin "turned the first spadeful of earth."[44]

The Board of Trustees for the new reformatory was determined to create a nonpunitive environment in which, it was believed, true rehabilitation could take place. "The new prison is not intended as a punitive institution, but as a corrective one," Wallace said. Even the name of the institution reflected this philosophy: "We are even taking care that no stigma is attached to the name of the institution—it will be known as the California Institution for Women."[45] Having taken several field trips to other women's reformatories around the country, the board suggested using the Federal Prison for Women, an isolated farm near Alderson, West Virginia, as a model and, what is more, sent the architectural drawings to "expert penologists all over the United States for criticism."[46] Emily Latham, another member of the board, wrote that the state had decided to provide "152 separate rooms for inmates and two dormitories which can care for eight each." She further explained that the prison was built on a ten-year building plan. As soon as money became available, there were to be additional cottages, a separate hospital unit, a recreation hall, and an "adequate" industrial building.[47]

The sponsors hoped that the institution would prove a successful implementation of women's-prison ideals. During the site selection controversy, board members argued that the remoteness of the chosen location was one of its desirable features. The isolation it provided would allow an institutional microcosm to develop—a "household"—and would obviate the need for walls or fences because the women would have no accessible place to which to escape. Unlike the early Folsom, this wall-less prison would need no guard posts. The isolation would effectively restrain the women. What was more, without the tangible symbols of imprisonment—walls, fences, or guards—the place might not feel so repressive to the inmates, increasing the chances of their rehabilitation. The board never had a chance to test this concept.

THE MEN ASSUME CONTROL

As attractive as the board's ideals were, Ulysses S. Webb, a Republican who had been serving as the state's attorney-general since 1902, ruled that their execution was unconstitutional. In July 1932, shortly after he had ruled that all employees at the new institution were to be qualified civil servants, Webb announced that, under his reading of the state constitution, the proposed removal of female prisoners was illegal on two counts. One, the women were serving prison, not reformatory sentences, and the new institution was inadequately secured to qualify as a prison. Two, the State Board of Prison Directors, he stated, governed the female prisoners of San Quentin and those prisoners, therefore, could not legally be moved from the state prison and delivered into the hands of the Board of Trustees of the California Institution for Women.[48]

Had no new law passed to address this decision, the women's institution would not have opened at all. There were many who were deeply disappointed that the women might not leave San Quentin, including the Board of Prison Directors, who had just finished proclaiming in their biennial report what a fine hospital the women's building would make. Members of the legislature also considered what a fine first-offenders prison the new Tehachapi complex would make as well, but it was necessary to house the women somewhere. Rather than allow the men to appropriate the new buildings, the institution's supporters backed a bill temporarily ceding its control to the men, while preserving its intended use. Introduced by Eleanor Miller, the bill declared the new site the Female Department of the State Prison at San Quentin at the California Institution for Women.[49]

Making the institution a branch of San Quentin meant returning control of it from a woman-dominated Board of Trustees to the Board of Prison Directors and the warden. In summer 1933, a man by the name of Hugh A. Smith became the institution's head, with the title deputy warden. His first tasks were to answer the attorney-general's objection to sending prison inmates to a reformatory and to erect a fence around the twelve-acre site on which the buildings stood. Built by San Quentin's road crew, the fence was made of ten-foot-high chain link topped by two feet of barbed wire. With this very visible testimony to their incarceration, the female inmates could occupy the facilities and, in November 1933, all 134 of them moved from San Quentin to Tehachapi. When Dr. Leo Stanley reflected on the women's departure from San Quentin, he wrote "It was all the Warden and I could do to keep from cheering . . . so glad were we to see the women leave." [50]

The women were full of anticipation and hope about their move. "We're on the trail of the rainbow!" wrote one female inmate for the November *Bulletin*. It was a "rainbow of hope" they sought, as she and the others were "released into another, newer form of incarceration." But even they did not give the ideals forming the place much of a chance. When they arrived, for example, the inmates found no locks on their cell doors and moved quickly to get that situation changed. One inmate, testifying later to a legislative committee, explained why: "When we came here from San Quentin, there were no locks on our doors, and we requested them for ourselves for our own protection from one another." [51]

The self-governing cottage system of residence was designed to be "campuslike," and to provide enough distinct units to make prisoner classification and segregation possible. A number of out-of-state observers, intrigued by the pastoral setting, came to inspect the results of the first round of building at Tehachapi. Just after the inmates' transfer, the *Christian Science Monitor* published several photographs of the prison's Normandy architecture and noted that some members of the legislature believed the institution's trustees and other sponsors had "allowed ideals to overrun reason." As intended, the "cells" were really private rooms, ten by eight feet, painted in colors, and the administration encouraged the inmates to decorate and personalize their rooms. Even before the administration changed, the first woman hired as superintendent had had her doubts that a prison was an appropriate place to decorate. She was quoted as saying, "I suppose the color is highly immoral, but I like it, and I think [the inmates] will, too." Another observer was clear that, for him, there was no decoration that could hide the reality of imprisonment. He wrote, "It is rather pitiful to see how the women prisoners have made their lonely rooms attractive." [52]

As it turned out, the women were to spend many idle hours in their rooms.

11 and 12. Two views of cells, or "dormitory" rooms, at the California Institute for Women at Tehachapi. The women had furnishings that included a bed, rocking chair, and dresser. (San Francisco Archives, San Francisco Public Library.)

The male administrators displayed no interest in pursuing the educational and vocational training programs the Board of Trustees had planned for the institution. The board had intended to have professional educators teach the inmates in many subjects, they had planned an eight-hour work day on the prison farm or in the prison industry for all of the inmates, and they had anticipated an expanded building program. None of this happened under male leadership. In fact, the inmates were more idle than they had been in their new building at San Quentin. "Last year, fresh vegetables perished unpicked while the women were held indoors or in little uncultivated walled courts in idleness and were forced to eat canned fruits and vegetables," asserted Emily Latham in an indignant statement to the press in March 1934.[53]

Even some of the equipment purchased for the prison went unused. Latham said that, "Laundry machinery costing $1000 lie in their crates. Yet it was bought so the women might be trained in the use of commercial laundry equipment." The enforced idleness of the inmates meant that they did not participate in any prison industry, even the flagmaking of San Quentin, and that they, too, were soon complaining of isolation and boredom. Pleading to the Prison Directors in March 1934, former board members, the president of the League of Women Voters, and others cried for relief for the Tehachapi inmates. With scandal threatening, they finally achieved the appointment of a female warden to replace Hugh Smith. The Prison Directors' action made Josephine Jackson the world's first deputy warden; this pleased Latham and Wallace only insofar as Jackson was a woman. They had wanted a specially trained penological expert to take the job, with the veteran Jackson remaining an assistant, but after more than a year of Smith's neglect, Latham called Jackson's appointment, "a distinct step forward." [54] That decision left men only as guards patrolling the fence, but resulted in few programmatic changes. [55]

WOMEN RESUME CONTROL

By autumn of 1934, in response to an unfavorable site visit of the Board of Prison Directors, some members of the legislature and some editorialists were calling the institution a failure, "unsatisfactory," "a mistake," a "total flop." Claims were that it was much more expensive to maintain than the ward at San Quentin had been, that it was overcrowded, unproductive, that the inmates were idle and miserable, and that it was way too expensive to maintain. The color and the decorative frills were an easy target for such criticism. Some called for its abandonment and the return of the inmates to San Quentin, a ploy Wallace quickly recognized as a way for the Prison Directors to turn the institution into "a prison for male first offenders." This attempt riled numerous women's organizations in the state, including the California Federation of Women's Clubs, the League of Women Voters, and the WCTU. In October, Governor Frank Merriam released a statement of support for the institution and for the creation of a board of trustees, composed this time entirely of women. [56] He said he would support legislation to this end.

The activist women of California welcomed Merriam's support, but they had already begun steps to by-pass the legislature and secure a constitutional amendment through the initiative process. A letter dated January 22, 1934, from the secretary of the Los Angeles League of Women Voters to the state office in Berkeley indicates that Latham had addressed the former group about supporting a ballot initiative. In another letter to the league's president, dated February 2, 1934, Latham explained that a constitutional amendment achieved through a ballot initiative would save at least two years over going through the legislature. Moreover, the initiative process would educate voters as to the problems of the women's prison.[57]

Support for the ballot initiative was not forthcoming in 1934, however, but the state senator from Kern County, J. L. Wagy, introduced a bill in January 1935; it passed in April 1935. Pending approval of the voters in November, this constitutional amendment provided for an institution for females convicted of felonies to be governed by a special board of the legislature's choosing, and allowed for treatment of the women to be different than that of men similarly convicted. The women's clubs of California waged a vigorous campaign to pass this amendment, with the National Council of Jewish Women, the Young Woman's Christian Association, the California Federation of Women's Clubs, the Women's Christian Temperance Union, and the League of Women Voters all endorsing it and disseminating educational materials in support of its passage.[58]

"Give the women this chance to make it work!" was the slogan, and a big part of the message was that a new, separate board would proceed with the original plans to professionalize the administration of Tehachapi. "The superintendent is not a skilled person," the literature read, "but a matron acting under the supervision of the warden at San Quentin." Countering the argument that the institution was too expensive, the handbills claimed that skilled administration would make the institution largely self-supporting in "a comparatively short time."[59] On November 3, 1935, the California electorate passed Senate Constitutional Amendment 21, and at last the women had their separate institution.

Members of the new Board of Trustees included Wallace, again as chair; Florence Gillis, active in the California Federation of Women's Clubs; Anna Law, the first state president of the League of Women Voters; and two men.[60] The legislature passed a bill granting the board parole powers and thus made its autonomy complete.

One of the first official acts that Wallace promised was the elimination of the "elaborate pillows and draperies and bric-a-brac" that adorned the prison and made it vulnerable to criticism. Another was hiring a "skilled" superintendent to replace Josephine Jackson. Florence Monahan was the board's choice. She was an attorney and "one of the best known penologists in the United States," who resigned her job as superintendent of the Illinois Training School for Girls to take the California post.[61] Monahan's appointment and Jackson's demotion represented the triumph of professional ideals over old-fashioned paternalistic (or maternalistic) prison management. With this appointment in 1936, the women of California finally assumed control over their fallen sisters, the female felons of California, at the California Institution for Women at Tehachapi.

With activist middle-class clubwomen taking the lead, California had achieved additional segregation in its prison system. Convicted women had a prison of their own. Many of the male legislators and prison administrators envied the women their prison farm, and determined that men should have at least equivalent facilities. The success of the women in their enterprise thus led directly to the long-sought reformatory for men.

5

Minimum Security for a Few Good Men,

1930–1944

Stone walls do not a prison make,
Nor iron bars a cage
From Richard Lovelace, "To Althea, From Prison"

Like the drive for a separate institution for women, the analogous drive for a reformatory institution for men deemed susceptible to rehabilitation achieved its first manifest success in the 1930s. Unlike the women's quest that began in the twentieth century, however, the opening of the California Institution for Men at Chino in July 1940 culminated a pursuit beginning among California reformers no later than 1866. In that year James Woodworth, secretary of the California Prison Commission, wrote of the need for a "house of correction" for reclaimable young criminals over the age of eighteen. Even before then, various legislative observers and prison board directors had observed the indiscriminate mixing of relatively young convicts with older, more vicious ones and had proclaimed the need for classification and separation within the institution at San Quentin. The men's movement even achieved legislative authorization before the women's did when, in 1911, the state passed "an act to establish the California State Reformatory," emulating other states, including the western ones of Washington and Utah.[1] Nonetheless, the state built no such institution until the end of the 1930s, and only then because an outraged legislature, an adamant and progressive warden, and new, supportive prison directors thwarted attempts from the executive office to defy the state's law by building another maximum security prison.

In the struggle to build Chino lay the historic ambivalence inherent in California's policy toward criminals. On the one hand, the public empathy for people caught defying society's rules dictated their humane treatment and corrective circumstances. On the other hand, public identification with the victims of crime and resentment toward lawbreakers dictated punitive institutions denying the humanity of the criminals. Seeing these two views as mutually exclusive, the fearful public, through its elected officials, again and again shied from investing in reform institutions. As with earlier reforms, achieving an industrial farm for criminal men took shocking public scandals that revealed the degradation resulting from denying the humanity of human beings. Unlike Tehachapi, which owed its existence to the persistence of pesky female reformers, Chino developed as an experiment in minimum security on the heels of a brutality and mismanagement scandal at San Quentin. In 1944 additional spilloff from that scandal, combined with the initial success of Chino and even Tehachapi, finally resulted in the first major overhaul of the California state prison system since its inception ninety years earlier.

REFORMATORY MOVEMENT IN
NINETEENTH-CENTURY CALIFORNIA

The California Prison Commission sent its secretary, James Woodworth to the National Prison Congress held in Cincinnati in October of 1870. Woodworth endorsed the findings of the congress and contributed to the dissemination of its "Declaration of Principles" by publishing the adopted resolutions in his annual report. A number of the thirty-seven articles addressed the basic reformatory principle that criminals are capable of becoming moral citizens. Article 11, for example, made "belief in the capability of the prisoner for reformation, on the part of prison officers, a necessity." Articles 3, 19, and 31, respectively, advocated the "progressive classification of prisoners, based on character"; the grading and classification of prisoners as well as prisoners and separate prisons "for women, and for criminals of the younger class"; and state-controlled prison systems consisting of "a graduated series of reformatory establishments." [2]

Serious overcrowding and deterioration at San Quentin gave the commission cause to think the legislature might act favorably on a proposal to establish a separate reformatory for young offenders, and so submitted such a bill in 1872. Had the commission's bill passed, the legislature would have authorized the construction at San Quentin of a distinct set of buildings to house at least four hundred convicted felons under the age of twenty-five. Before failing passage, however, the bill had been amended to place the new facility on the state-owned land at Folsom. Even the California Prison Commission protested this possibility; Secretary Woodworth claimed that the granite quarries and intense heat associated with the Folsom location could only suit an institution of punishment, not of reformation.[3]

The state had purchased the Folsom site in 1858 expecting eventually to evacuate San Quentin entirely and to start afresh at a place where granite quarrying was possible.[4] Because of limited funding, the construction there of a branch prison rather than a reformatory seemed to render the reformatory movement a serious blow for some time to come. Any reform designed to remedy the persistent evil of mingling convicts regardless of age and crime called for some expenditure on additional prison buildings. In the absence of a reformatory, prison directors and the warden renewed their calls for an immediate program to build cells for all inmates, but this expenditure also did not occur.[5]

Reformers nonetheless continued to espouse the principles of the National Congress. California held its own congress in 1881, when the Prison Reform Convention of California met in San Francisco. Much of the discussion there concerned the political appointment of prison personnel and the ongoing controversy over prison labor competing with free labor. When the focus turned to moral reformation of the convicts, California's Golden Age penologists repeatedly resolved the apparent conflict between the punitive and reformatory functions of the prison in the same way: the custodial institution was to be the second family for inmates who, it was assumed, issued from broken or failed homes. One particular address to the convention, endorsed and disseminated by both the California Prison Commission and Governor George C. Perkins, expressed this philosophy very clearly: "Under this system," the speaker claimed, "the administrative officer represents the father of a family of from twelve to twenty-four boys, whom he regulates, encourages or represses, and influences for good."[6]

In order to provide this second family for male convicts, the state needed to train qualified personnel, to effect a classification system, and to build an appropriate physical plant. Several times around the turn of the century the legislature heard the suggestion that even the existing physical plant could form the basis for a segregated system. In its 1893–94 report, for example, the Board of Prison Directors recommended turning Folsom into an industrial prison for youthful and first offenders, and that San Quentin become an institution for recidivists.[7] Some expenditures were required to accomplish this end, because additional housing and training facilities would distinguish the reformatory from the prison.

The legislature was not forthcoming with the funds. Moreover, the state's prison experts changed their mind as to which institution should become the moderate one. One report made to the assembly on March 10, 1903, by the Select Committee on State Prisons and Reformatory Institutions recommended the passage of an act making Folsom the recipient of all repeat offenders. In 1904, making its first report since its creation as an oversight body for all of the state's institutions, the Board of Charities and Corrections recommended building eight hundred new separate cells at Folsom, transferring there all of the "hardened" criminals housed at San Quentin, and then converting San Quentin into a prison for the "younger and better class of prisoners." The legislature finally made this suggestion law in 1917, but only after a brutality scandal and a failed attempt at a separate reformatory intervened.[8]

THE FIRST STATE REFORMATORY

The brutality scandal of 1904 and 1905, which resulted in the dismissal of Warden Tompkins and public support for the Progressive-era solutions such as parole reform, also brought about the first legislative action to build a reformatory and thus bring the California prison system up to East Coast standards. In the years immediately following the revelations, a number of reform measures underscored the optimism of those years: John Hoyle, a humane man trained in penology, took over the warden's job at San Quentin; the legislature authorized expenditures for new facilities at both San Quentin and Folsom; and Governor George Pardee appointed a new board of prison directors, consisting of men with progressive ideas. One of these appointees, a former judge named Tirey Ford became the president of the Board of Directors and, in 1910, wrote and published a history of the state's prisons in order to gain sympathy for an environmental theory of criminality and for a new building program. "The problem of modern penology," he wrote "is to segregate those susceptible of becoming good citizens—who are largely found among the first offenders—and make good citizens of them." It was in this atmosphere of hope that the legislature, in 1909, finally authorized the prison directors to collect the data necessary for the building of a state reformatory.[9]

The directors' study resulted in a detailed report on a "proposed reformatory for adult offenders," dated December 1910; the report contained the responses to queries of reformatory administrators elsewhere, floor plans of other institutions, and the proposed text for authorizing legislation. Success for the reformatory advocates seemed to come the following year when, based on modifications of the directors' recommendations, the legislature passed "an act to establish the California State Reformatory."[10] Under the supervision of the Board of Prison Directors, the state reformatory, like San Quentin and Folsom, was to accept male first offenders between the ages of sixteen and thirty, and the principle of the indeterminate sentence was to apply to each of the inmates. These rules emulated the model reformatory at Elmira, New York, and allowed for the release of an inmate when the prison directors had adjudged him reformed. Requiring a purchase of at least six hundred agriculturally sound acres and buildings to accommodate at least one thousand inmates, the act appropriated $150,000 for immediate expenditure and commissioned the governor, the lieutenant governor, and three unnamed others to find and purchase the necessary land.

The commission did, in fact, purchase twenty-seven hundred acres in Napa County, near Yountsville, and almost immediately local residents protested, predicting that the nearby presence of a reformatory would threaten both their personal safety and their property values. A sensitive legislature allowed the issue to lie fallow before appropriating any more funds for the project, and soon the Great War intervened and the progressive mood of the policymakers shifted. While awaiting a reformatory that might never happen, in 1917 the legislature took the oft-recommended step of distinguishing between the existing institutions by making Folsom the ultimate destination for repeat offenders and San Quentin the prison for first offenders. This action sealed the fate of the Napa County reformatory project; the next official attention it received was a 1921 repeal of the 1911 act. The state turned the land over to the Department of Finance to sell.[11] California still had no reformatory for youthful first offenders and no way to make the San Quentin plant serve the purpose.

THE SECOND REFORMATORY

While the male prison population had dropped below three thousand during the years of World War I, the 1920s saw a great increase in the population of both Folsom and San Quentin, straining the already tight facilities and the new probation system. By 1926, the two prisons housed more than fifty-two hundred male inmates, and in 1927 the legislature finally responded to deteriorating conditions by authorizing an investigation into the feasibility of building a new prison somewhere in Southern California. The idea was to save the expense and the danger of transporting prisoners from the increasingly populous southern regions of the state. Two years later, in 1929, the investigators had not yet found an appropriate property, but the legislature voted to continue the search.[12]

That same legislature also heeded the urgent calls of its Crime Commission to create separate institutions for women and for young male first offenders. In response, another two acts passed, authorizing the establishment of each kind of institution.[13] In three separate 1929 acts, therefore, the legislature appropriated the following: in April, $1,000 to continue the search for a Southern California prison site; in May, $475,000 to establish a prison for women; and in June, $375,000 to establish a reformatory for male first offenders between the ages of eighteen and twenty-four. This latter act authorized the appointment of a five-member commission to find a suitable location, and this body apparently superseded the one seeking a Southern California site for an undefined type of prison.

In addition to appropriating unprecedented funds for the creation of separate and graduated penal institutions, the 1929 legislature made an attempt to reform penal administration. A Department of Penology, headed by a director of penology, resulted from a desire to meld professional penology into the state government. With no staff of its own, however, the department really only functioned as a liaison between the governor's office and five separate and autonomous divisions: 1) the Division of Prisons and Paroles, under the auspices of the Board of Prison Directors; 2) the Division of Pardons and Commutations, under the Advisory Pardon Board; 3) the Division of Criminology, under the new California Crime Commission; 4) the Division of Criminal Identification, under the Bureau of Criminal Identification and Investigation; and 5) the Division of Narcotic Enforcement.[14] While it was unclear what the legislature specifically wanted the new "department" to accomplish, its creation signified a sentiment for integrating professional criminology into the state's prison system.

In spite of the legislature's support for both a women's prison and an adult male reformatory, the only successful search committee was the one authorized in May to find a suitable site for a women's prison. In July of 1930, that committee bought more than sixteen hundred acres in Kern County, and almost immediately the purchase spurred controversy. Opponents in the legislature suggested that the Kern County site was both a poor and an extravagant choice. After some acrimonious exchanges, an official examining committee vindicated the purchase, declaring it an excellent site. The controversy, however, may have made the other searchers shy of arid Southern California locations. This would have complicated the task of the committee seeking a men's reformatory site, since this committee adopted the earlier goal of locating in the southern portion of the state.[15]

In fact, the committee did not agree on a choice at all. Failure to spend the appropriations after four years meant the money allocated for the young men's prison project reverted to the state treasury. This happened in June of 1933, almost a year after the attorney general had ruled that the new women's prison could not operate under the jurisdiction of the Board of Trustees and just as the Tehachapi prison reverted to the control of the Board of Prison Directors and was declared a branch of San Quentin.

For the next two years, the fate of the women's prison was in doubt and, during that time, while more verbal support for the men's reformatory issued from advisory sources, nothing was done to further the project. Vocal advocates of a reformatory included two members of the new Board of Prison Terms and Paroles, which administered parole and the new indeterminate sentence law. Around 1934, when the depression made job-finding difficult even for men without criminal records, Warren H. Atherton and Frank C. Sykes, both of the parole board, publicly urged the segregation and training of young male first offenders.[16] Their voices, of course, carried no authority; even the newly established director of penology, who nominally oversaw the various prison boards, had no policymaking power in what was a very haphazard and increasingly ad hoc administrative structure. Official legislative action on the reformatory project awaited a legal decision on the fate of Tehachapi.

When the Prison Directors took control of the women's prison, the board abandoned planned allocations for buildings and vocational programs. Soon the forlorn and idle female inmates complained of isolation, and the project's legislative opponents talked of abandoning the site and even of sending the women back to San Quentin.[17] In October 1934, Governor Frank Merriam announced his support for the Tehachapi experiment, and in January of 1935, state Senator James Wagy of Bakersfield, Kern County, introduced a constitutional amendment to give control over the women's prison to a separate Board of Trustees. Passage of this amendment ensured the women's claim to the Tehachapi site, and so it was after the legislature voted to put the amendment on the November ballot that another "act to establish the Southern California Prison" passed.[18] The sequence and circumstances strongly suggest that the policymakers waited to see whether they could obtain the site of the women's industrial farm for a new men's reformatory before proceeding with the additional expense of buying a second such prison site in Southern California.

BUILDING A PRISON AT CHINO

Had it not been for another brutality scandal breaking at San Quentin and the revelations of blatant executive disregard for legislative intent, the California Institution for Men at Chino might have become another maximum security prison. The 1935 act to establish the Southern California prison was the third legislative authorization since 1911 to build a reformatory. While this act set no age standards for inmates, it did specify that the new prison would accept only male felons adjudged "capable of reformation," in keeping with the law's purpose, "to provide for segregation from hardened criminals of offenders of a mild type." The bill set aside four hundred thousand dollars for the purchase of a suitable farm site and instructed the Board of Prison Directors to establish institutional rules and selection processes designed to "restore [prisoners] to freedom as self-supporting and self-respecting members of the State." [19]

Among those on the site-selection commission were the governor, then Frank Merriam, and A. R. O'Brien, then president of the Board of Prison Directors. They quickly purchased a twenty-six-hundred-acre sugar beet farm near Chino in San Bernardino County, on which they promised local residents—in explicit defiance of legislative intent—that the state would definitely build a maximum security institution.[20] Those promises occurred as early as 1937, the same year State Architect George McDougall had apparently produced plans for an industrial farm institution and also the same year the legislature allocated two million dollars to complete the first phase of building that institution.[21] On January 11, 1937, McDougall wrote a memorandum describing his understanding of the legislature's intended institution. Of the style, he wrote, "The exterior appearance is to be pleasing . . . and is to convey more the idea that it is a school than a prison or bastile." Of the embattlements, he wrote, "There will be no enclosing wall." And of the housing arrangements, he wrote, "Good behavior may be rewarded by advancement from . . . one kind of housing to another . . . from a single detention cell to a dormitory." Governor Merriam assessed these ideas with a phrase that, according to his own account, he used frequently, "You want a clubhouse instead of a prison." [22]

Subversion of the state architect's plans occurred when Governor Merriam, not wanting to build a "clubhouse" for criminals, suggested turning the project over to an independent architectural firm. The Board of Prison Directors apparently supported alterations to the state architect's conception in its resolution issued August 4, 1937, that "a prison of the medium security type should be constructed . . . [and] also that additional provisions should be made for the construction of a certain number of maximum security, classification, and detention cells to permit the housing of all types of prisoners." In December 1937, as the authorized contracting party, the Board of Prison Directors hired the private architectural firm of Walker and Eisen to carry out these notions, and also to gain as much New Deal federal assistance as possible. Walker and Eisen, who, until caught in a serious financial bind for not meeting state prison goals, directed the construction of an institution very different from a reformatory.[23]

As Walker and Eisen later testified, they did not directly know of the legislature's intent for Chino, nor were they entirely clear on the architectural distinctions between minimum, medium, and maximum security. They did, however, know that the governor and the board wanted the prison to look like a prison, and they spent most of the allocated funds building gun towers, maximum security cells with heavy iron doors, and a formidable administration building. In the end, this left housing for only 440 prisoners instead of the 1,100 which the law established as the minimum capacity of the institution. Moreover, the expected Public Works Administration funds were not forthcoming. In 1937 the federal Prison Industries Reorganization Administration, at the request of Governor Merriam, had studied the California prisons and endorsed the erection of a reformatory at the Chino site. Ironically, because the PWA concluded that the actual institution under construction "did not meet the need of the penal system in California," the change in plans meant no federal funds.[24]

The subversion of legislative intent occurred because the legislature simply was not paying attention as the governor and the Board of Prison Directors proceeded according to their own agenda. As to whether the board thought it necessary to carry out the wishes of the legislature, Chairman A. R. O'Brien testified at a legislative hearing in 1941 that, "If the Legislature had an idea that I knew was wrong, I wouldn't go for it, I would go for my own idea."[25]

REMOVING THE "OLD" PRISON BOARD

The legislature came to life, though, when news broke on March 21, 1939, of a "hunger strike" at San Quentin, and solons reacted to the specter of thousands of crowded, abused prisoners raging out of control. One of the legislature's first actions, ten days later, was to endorse the contract between the state and Walker and Eisen in an effort to complete the construction of the Southern California Prison as soon as possible and to relieve some of San Quentin's overcrowding.[26] At the same time, the new governor, Culbert Olson, launched an investigation into the conditions at San Quentin leading to the strike. The egregious mismanagement he found there spurred the legislature to investigate the other responsibilities of the Board of Prison Directors, including the delays in the completion of Chino. Both of these investigations revealed serious flaws in a prison system where an unpaid board of directors had responsibility but no real control, and where absence of

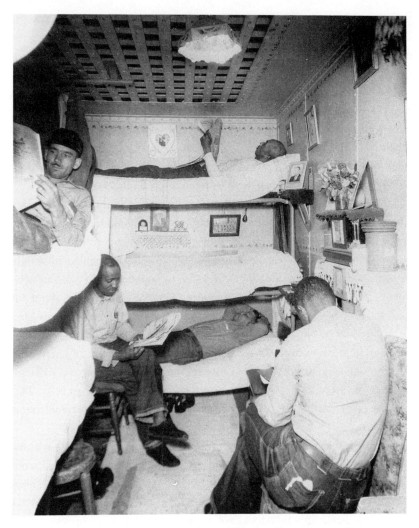

13. Typical "tank" above the condemned row cells in San Quentin, 1935. This picture shows five men in a cell measuring 7′8″ x 11′8″ x 7′11″, with no toilet facilities. (San Francisco Archives, San Francisco Public Library.)

leadership fostered inhumane conditions and a nightmare of violence. In the immediate wake of such horror, the legislature was finally ready for change.

The governor's investigation of conditions at San Quentin soon turned into a trial, heard by Governor Olson, pitting the state against the Board of Prison Directors: A. R. O'Brien, T. N. Harvey, Edward L. Abbott, Donald

Kolts, and John D. McGilvray. Charges filed in October 1939 accused the directors of misconduct, incompetency, and neglect of duty.[27] Before the end of the hearings in the spring of 1940, Olson's court had accumulated five volumes of transcribed testimony, much of it revealing stories of wanton brutality, commencing with the board's appointment of Court Smith as San Quentin's warden in April of 1936. This was a time when the system's male inmate census hovered around nine thousand and a prison escape had recently occurred. Rather than assume leadership, however, Smith had fearfully hid from the prisoners and had presided over their violent repression. The prison directors were charged with looking the other way.

Smith, a former policeman, had spent eight years as warden of Folsom, where he had gained a reputation for being stern and aloof. The board had appointed him to succeed Warden James Holohan, a decent man by all accounts, who for eight years had had his reform efforts stymied by a tight legislature and who was kidnapped and shot in January of 1935 as four prisoners effected their escape. The prisoners were "apprehensive" about the new warden, but an interview with him in the *Bulletin*, dated March–April 1936, announced optimistically that "above all else he radiated an air of kindness and understanding toward the inmate and his problems," and predicted, "There can be no doubt that upon entering a new era, San Quentin will continue to progress and continue to be a tolerable city behind walls."[28] That was the last issue of the *Bulletin*, which had been in continuous publication since 1913.

Smith's fear of the inmates was almost palpable, and he dealt with it by not dealing with them. He, in fact, refused to enter the prison alone. Eliminating the prisoners' publication was another way to make them disappear. A more literal way was to banish as many as possible to the dungeon cells, barred, unfurnished cells in a fifty-foot cave, resonating as loudly as any other symbol at San Quentin of the Dark Ages. Ironically, Smith had announced on his arrival abolition of the dungeon, and yet he used it extensively. Men sent there were left for weeks on end without beds or blankets or food, except at the whim of the guards.[29]

Rather than the dungeon, the hunger strikers in March of 1939 had been sent to solitary cells, where part of the regimen was a torture Warden Smith had introduced to the prison: standing on "the spot." The spot was a circle, twenty-two inches in diameter, where the prisoners were forced to stand all day or suffer beatings. Beatings occurred regularly anyway, and some of the

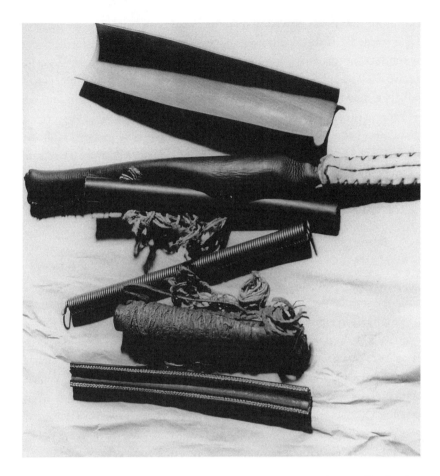

14. Weapons used to beat prisoners, showing a spring in the butt end of a strap. Displayed at a legislative hearing, 1939. (San Francisco Archives, San Francisco Public Library.)

more sadistic guards used a lead-shot-loaded hose as a weapon.[30] Faced with the revelation of these and more atrocities, even the most convict-hating newspaper editorialists could not find a justification for such behavior and, at best, resorted to denial and disbelief.

The members of the Board of Prison Directors found no justification for these outrages either, but, when they were charged with responsibility for them, they pleaded they had none. They claimed that, in fact, it was only their responsibility to hire a warden and not their responsibility to ensure his competence. The attorney defending the board found in the following syllogism proof that it was absurd to hold the board responsible for the actions of the warden: "If the Board ever sought to remove a warden for neglect, misconduct, or incompetency, then the same Board would probably have to remove itself because it would find that there was a warden guilty of neglect, and since they had appointed the warden, they would have to turn around and remove themselves." [31]

Not surprisingly, the governor rejected this argument, found the directors guilty of neglect of duty, and dismissed them. The legislature passed an amendment to the state constitution in 1940 that precluded future use of this argument by explicitly granting the board "the power to remove the Wardens and Clerks for misconduct, incompetency, or neglect of duty." [32]

THE NEW BOARD

While the scandal put in motion efforts to remodel the entire prison system, Governor Olson's first act after dismissing the old board was to appoint a new one. The disgraced head of the old board, A. R. O'Brien, vowed to take his case to the supreme court, but meanwhile Olson empowered a new chairman, Isaac Pacht, a former judge from Los Angeles and a man with known sentiments for prison reform. The first acts the new board undertook were designed to ameliorate conditions at the overcrowded prisons. The board voted to install a cafeteria system at San Quentin so that the inmates could have hot food and to investigate the possibility of installing radio earphones in individual cells at both San Quentin and Folsom. [33]

At this first meeting in July of 1940, the new directors also appointed an acting warden to San Quentin before officially dismissing Court Smith. The first of the reforming wardens the new board was to choose was Clinton Duffy, whose father had been a guard at San Quentin, who had grown up there, worked in various administrative positions, and who saw this appointment as the fulfillment of a lifelong dream. Not knowing whether his appointment would become permanent (it did), Duffy, in thirty days, did everything he could think to do to bring humane conditions to San Quentin. His first acts were symbolic: he had the bars ripped out of the dungeon; he appointed a new cook who had instructions to buy and use plenty of high quality food, including beef; he eliminated the policy of shaving the heads of new arrivals; and he abolished the prisoners' numbered shirts. Smith tendered his resignation the day the new board appointed Duffy, but stubbornly stayed at his desk for those first thirty days.[34]

The final act the new board took during its first meeting was to initiate an investigation into the completion of the new prison at Chino, hoping to relieve San Quentin and Folsom of at least five hundred inmates within thirty days. Chino, of course, was nowhere near completion, nor was it being built to accommodate the anticipated number of inmates. While the board, and subsequently the legislature, investigated the Chino situation, the new prison directors sought a warden for the institution who would bring enlightened ideas to prison management. In December of 1940, Judge Pacht contacted Kenyon Scudder, who had once been a probation officer in Los Angeles and who had been working as a warden in a federal prison in Ohio.[35] Scudder, a trained penologist, had firm ideas about the kind of prison in which he would work and, according to his memoirs, he found the new directors daring to agree with him. With their backing, Scudder managed to establish Chino as a reformatory after all.

CHINO AS A REFORMATORY

Scudder made some demands on both the governor and the board before accepting even a temporary appointment as warden of Chino. Of the governor he demanded autonomy in choosing the prison's staff. It had long been true in California that governors used prison jobs as political rewards, even though penologists had decried that practice since the 1870 National Congress, and even though California had nominally eliminated it in the state's second constitution in 1879. Before accepting the Chino job, Scudder informed Governor Olson that he required a free hand in personnel selection.[36] Although Scudder subsequently confronted an unwanted Olson appointee, he successfully asserted his autonomy and, generally, the board supported him in developing a high level of personnel criteria. Prison personnel, Scudder thought, were key to the attainment of reformatory goals. Young first offenders needed teaching and encouragement to counteract the sense of worthlessness that motivated their destructive behavior, and only self-confident personnel could reliably treat the convicts with the requisite sympathy rather than contempt. Scudder was to be called the institution's superintendent rather than warden, and the men who worked directly with the inmates were to be supervisors rather than guards. For these supervisors, Scudder chose young, mostly college-educated men who had scored high on qualifying examinations. He then had certified instructors train them in sociology, psychology, philosophy, and, for self-defense, judo. They were not otherwise to be armed. For the most part, he faced no political interference, and Scudder chose fifty such men to open the institution.[37]

Of the board, Scudder demanded support for a physical plant as consistent with the reformatory philosophy as possible, given that some fortress-type structures had already been built. The new board had not challenged the way Chino was physically taking shape before offering Scudder the warden's position. In fact, the new directors seemed ignorant of the way their predecessors had allowed subversion of the state's reformatory plans. Rather, they had as their primary concern the quick availability of more room to hold prisoners. After Scudder received the job offer, he journeyed to Chino and saw the maximum security fortress being built there. Three of the planned ten gun towers already stood in place, a twenty-foot concrete wall was underway, and a massive administration building dominated the premises.[38] Only forty thousand dollars of the over $2 million budget remained at the time of Scudder's appointment, and there were rooms, with heavy cell doors, for less than half the anticipated number of inmates. Moreover, there were virtually no facilities for carrying on the activities of an industrial farm, the intended heart of the reformatory's activities.[39]

Seeing the institution's design as contradictory to the reformatory ideal, Scudder informed the board that he would not take the warden's job if the remaining forty thousand dollars went to complete the towers and a wall. He argued that, in a tangible way, the reformatory worked by being an open institution; the openness confronted the inmates on a daily basis with the need to exercise their heretofore underused ability to make responsible choices. Every day they chose not to leave an open institution represented a strengthening of their ability to function in a larger society full of analogous, if less concrete, restrictions. The board listened to these arguments and recognized that they represented a democratic departure from the popular view that Governor Merriam had expressed in his "clubhouse" description—the view that removing a criminal from freedom was not punishment enough. Daringly, the board concurred with Scudder. In the board's report, Director George Briggs coined the phrase that officially became the guiding principle of Chino and subsequent like institutions: "There can be no regeneration except in freedom." [40]

In accordance with the new philosophy, the board stopped construction of the gun towers and cement wall. A cyclone fence, erected as much to keep intruders out as to keep inmates in, defined the perimeter of the building complex. The prisoners used the completed portion of the wall as a handball court. In his memoirs and taped oral history reflections, Scudder said that he never admonished new arrivals against escape. Rather, he told them how to do it—by throwing a jacket over the barbed wire topping the fence—and, further, he informed them that their dormitory rooms would not be locked. [41] There were to be no armed guards preventing escape, either. The inmates' only inhibition to leaving the prison was to be a combination of their own restraint and the knowledge that they would be sent to San Quentin or Folsom on capture. In other words, Scudder challenged the inmates to make their own choices about their future. In doing so, ironically, escape became the measure of success or failure for Chino, just as it was for San Quentin and Folsom. The difference was that at Chino, escape, or lack of it, was to reflect the success of internal rather than external restraints.

Even without building the unwanted barricades, the remaining forty thousand dollars was inadequate to complete enough dormitory space to house the intended number of men. Judge Pacht went before the joint investigative committee in early 1941, asking for eight hundred thousand dollars to build enough dormitory units to house fifteen hundred men and, in addition, five hundred thousand dollars to initiate the farm program. The legislative committee boldly endorsed the Chino experiment as Scudder and the new Board of Prison Directors conceived of it, and by legislative enactment that year the prison gained a new, more innocuous name, the California Institution for Men. Even so, subsequent funding was adequate only for construction of temporary frame barracks. By the end of 1943, the state's capital investment in the Chino facilities exceeded $3.7 million, yet more than one-fourth of the 422 beds available then were in these temporary structures. [42]

The barracks and the new name were in place as the first thirty-four arrivals from San Quentin disembarked from a Greyhound bus on July 10, 1941. Scudder and his assistants had carefully chosen these transferees from among the quiet, "forgotten men" of San Quentin, and four hundred others were to follow that year. [43] Criteria for transfer were not scientific, and were honed over the next decade, but Scudder insisted that race not be a factor. If anything, he sought a racially integrated institution—the opposite of San Quentin, where de facto segregation was practiced, and Folsom, where segregation in celling and dining were de jure. Among the very first group of Chino inmates, Scudder had chosen "negroes, Mexicans, Filipinos, Japanese, and Caucasians."[44] To find suitable men, regardless of race, Scudder asked San Quentin personnel for recommendations. Few were forthcoming, Scudder postulated, because the prison management did not want to lose the more functional and pleasant inmates. He and his assistants found many of the transfers by combing the sometimes skimpy personal inmate files and by interviewing each of the candidates.

On the arrival of the first group that night in July of 1941, Scudder found himself experiencing doubt about his choices and even about the wisdom of the minimum security program. But, by that time, after seventy years of reformers agitating for a separate prison for tractable male convicts, the great experiment was on.[45] California had at last put in place enough separate institutions to constitute a prison system: San Quentin served as the main prison, Folsom as the prison for recidivists, Tehachapi as the women's prison, and now Chino filled a gap as the state's adult male reformatory. All that remained was devising a method to manage this system.

CHAPTER

6

Reforming the System, 1941–1944

. . . the hideous prison-wall
still hems him round and round
From Oscar Wilde, "The Ballad of Reading Gaol"

The 1941 legislature was eager to endorse the minimum security experiment at Chino, but the solons remained dismayed about the money the Merriam administration had wasted on unnecessary and unwanted buildings and on the cavalier disregard for legislative intent evident at the executive level. The collected penological literature from the previous seventy years had not persuaded the legislature to impose scientific, professional order on the state's prisons, but the revelations of 1939–40 came during an era characterized by such reform. The purpose of establishing so many New Deal agencies at the federal level and, subsequently, at the state level was to ensure that career bureaucrats had responsibility to effect government policy. In California, Democrat Culbert Olson had defeated incumbent Merriam in November 1938 by running as a New Deal candidate, and by the time Earl Warren won election in 1942, a system of government management in many realms was settling into place.[1] Change and reform were a part of the milieu in which news of prison neglect and mismanagement became public.

What these scandals revealed was the absence of clear lines of authority. Where the legislature had thought the Prison Directors were clearly responsible—in the supervision of the prisons—the directors had not recognized any responsibility, and soon uncontrolled violence terrorized San Quentin. On the other hand, where the legislature had thought that the directors had no discretionary authority—in determining the kind of new prison California was to build—they had assumed responsibility and overridden the expressed wishes of the legislature. The March 1941 report of the joint committee investigating Chino urged the fruition of the original reformatory goals, but more important, announced the need for an overhaul of the system. The report concluded, "There can be no solution of California's penal problem until archaic provisions which divide responsibility are replaced by a unified program administered by a single authority."[2] Indeed, even the titular office of director of penology had not been filled since 1933.

This need for someone to be in charge translated into a constitutional amendment that passed that same year. A new section of the article dealing with state institutions permitted the legislature to create a new government agency to take charge of "all institutions for all persons convicted of felonies."[3] This was the enabling clause that preceded bureaucratic reform, and it passed as part of the state's recovery from the prison scandals.

Some legislative and public healing from those scandals occurred during the time required to investigate the way to establish a new prison authority. During the height of the scandals, the warden, prison board, and governor had been cast as villains, and the criminals were seen more as victims themselves. In part, this temporary shift in the assignment of villainy accounted for support for the Chino experiment, and to the extent that it did, the embracing of the minimum security institution did not represent a more fundamental change in social attitudes toward criminals. A politically savvy Earl Warren, who ran for governor in 1942, had his own perspective on crime problems from his years of experience as a district attorney and, since 1939, as the state's attorney general. Prison-system reorganization was high on his political agenda. His experience told him that prison reform only occurred in the wake of a full-blown scandal and those of 1939 and 1940 had already receded in the public memory. So, to ensure support for his program, Warren awaited another opportunity to engage the public in his cause. Significantly, he chose an opportunity to engage their outrage at crime and their fear of criminals rather than their sympathy.[4]

Early in his first term, the chief of police of San Francisco informed Warren that a notorious armed robber, Lloyd Sampsell, part of the slick gang known as the "Yacht Bandits" who had plied and plundered the California coast, had more than once been spied "nightclubbing" in the city's North Beach area when he was supposed to be behind cell bars. Warren, who had helped send Sampsell to Folsom for a fifteen-year-to-life sentence, saw his opportunity here, and asked the chief to arrange for the press to be on hand when he arrested Sampsell during one of his nights out on the town. The chief and the press both obliged and caught Sampsell on November 26, 1943, at his lover's San Francisco apartment. Great public furor ensued. Within three days, on November 29, 1943, on the heels of the shocking news of a convicted prisoner enjoying his freedom, Warren chose his own committee, headed by Julian Alco, Warren's appointee to the prison board, to investigate penal affairs in the state.[5] It was to be the final investigating committee before the reorganization in 1944.

Given even more impetus by publicity surrounding a four-man escape from San Quentin the day after Christmas in 1943, the committee studied the operations at Folsom, San Quentin, Chino, and even Tehachapi, as well as the reform schools. The resulting report emphasized a lack of discipline at the men's institutions, even at Chino. The system of con-bosses—much like the trusties of Estell's day, where prisoners rather than staff ran various departments—prevailed at Folsom and, to a lesser extent, at San Quentin. Sampsell, an intelligent and articulate man, had been one of the favored prisoners; as a con-boss keeping the books at a wartime harvest camp near Oroville, Sampsell lived in a separate bunkhouse, one-quarter of a mile from the main camp. He had great freedom of movement and had taken to visiting San Francisco on weekends and returning to work on Sundays. Since he came and went at will, the prison that was to be his keeper was clearly malfunctioning. The committee found that con-bosses like Sampsell virtually ran Folsom. And San Quentin, although much more humane since Duffy took the wardenship, was also lax in discipline and favored the "bonarues," a term coined in California prisons indicating "easy street."[6] Resentment of con-bosses was great among fellow prisoners and the general public as well, and the discovery of their existence led to a cry for discipline.

Chino had no con-bosses, but the governor's committee remarked ruefully on the lack of discipline there, too. Smoking under "no smoking" signs, gambling, and familiarity with supervisors all led the committee to emphasize the need for respect for rules even in this open institution. Apparently some of the inmates agreed, and their council encouraged selection of new inmates only among those who had been at San Quentin for at least six months, or

15. Inmates in T-shirts outside the administration building at the California Institute for Men at Chino, 1942. This photograph was labeled "far cry from grim." (San Francisco Archives, San Francisco Public Library.)

long enough to appreciate the relative freedom of Chino.[7] The committee agreed that a real classification system was necessary to make Chino work, and that Scudder, even though he was running the country's most open institution deserved continuing support. One observer suggested, however, that had it not been the war years, Scudder would have lost his job because of some of his blunders at Chino; one example was the first-degree murderer Scudder brought down from San Quentin for his gymnastic abilities who effected a quick and easy escape to Canada.[8]

As it was, the committee was not so much concerned with hiring and firing, especially of well-meaning personnel, but with preparing the system to withstand the increase in prison population that the war's end would surely bring. The system needed tightening. It needed reorganization.

Even before the governor's committee made this recommendation, Warren himself promised to hold the Board of Prison Directors responsible for all prison mismanagement, and in January of 1944 he announced his plan to replace the prison board with a permanent, professional, nonpartisan direc-

16. Kenyon Scudder in the west "dormitory" of the California Institute for Men at Chino, 1941. Scudder's title was executive superintendent rather than warden. (San Francisco Archives, San Francisco Public Library.)

tor of corrections.[9] Members of Olson's prison board, including Isaac Pacht and George Briggs, fought the change, with Pacht saying, "I don't believe a few escapes warrant complete reorganization of the prison system."[10] He favored hiring a general business manager. Members of the Board of Prison Terms, whose functions under Warren's plan would transfer to a professional three-person Adult Authority, also protested. Warden Duffy of San Quentin, whose job was on the line as Warren and his committee questioned his competence, and Supervisor Scudder of Chino both testified to the legislature on behalf of the existing system of administration.[11]

Governor Warren insisted, however, that "scandal after scandal" showed the existing prison system to be "structurally unsound," and it needed reorganization if, as he put it, "we are going to make progress." With a few compromise amendments worked out in the wee hours, the governor got his way on January 29, 1944.[12]

The 1941 constitutional amendment had made reorganization possible, and a 1944 statute, passed during an extra session of the legislature, made it actual.[13] This act stripped the State Board of Prison Directors of its authority over prison management and placed that authority in a Department of Corrections, headed by a Director of Corrections, who was to be a trained penologist removable, if necessary, by the governor after a hearing by the newly created Board of Corrections. The Board of Trustees of the California Institute for Women lost some of its powers, too, as the department assumed responsibility for the "care, custody, treatment, training, discipline, and employment of inmates."[14] The old boards were to remain as advisors while the director was to coordinate the activities of all of the state's penal institutions.

Finally, someone was in charge of the prison system. In this case, that person was Richard A. McGee, experienced in corrections in several states, who retained his post as director of corrections until his retirement, more than twenty-three years later.

Thus, the prison scandals that combined to permit experimentation with minimum security at Chino also led to a major overhaul of the loose prison system. In the process, some change in the general view of prisoners as desperate fiends came about so that even a committee charged with fixing a system that allowed escape still supported the Chino experiment as one "worthy in concept." Perhaps more significant was the establishment the following year of still another prison. This was to be neither a minimum security prison nor a maximum security prison, but a medium security prison, designed to provide farm opportunities and industrial and vocational training, but with more external restraints than Chino had and far fewer than those of either Folsom or San Quentin.[15] The state built this compromise prison at Soledad.

While these changes did not represent a revolution in California's prison system, they certainly put into place, for the first time, a structure through which to interpret and effect penological thinking. Since the system began, there was a perceived need to separate prisoners from each other and to classify them according to their predicted ability to return to society as functioning citizens. As long as the state's only prisons were the strongholds of

Folsom and San Quentin, prisoners were all, in effect, treated alike. It took an evolving view of prisoners as individuals to allow an experiment at the opposite extreme—the open prison at Chino. Its success, even crudely measured by its survival, forever changed the unidimensional view of prisoners only as desperate beings. Soledad, the moderate institution, did not represent a retreat from the message of Chino, but, instead, a place where the state could send still other kinds of individual prisoners, those determined able to reform, but needing more guidance and tangible restraint than Chino could provide. By the mid-1940s, the California prison system was set on a new course of integrating criminals into the larger society.

EPILOGUE

In light of the dramatic changes in California's prisons that had occurred since the turn of the century, a 1954 senate committee planning for future correctional needs assumed the system would undergo continual movement. "Certainly the experience of the past 50 years has amply demonstrated that whatever the needs for places of imprisonment may be in the year 2000, *the prisons built today will not be the right answer* [italics in original]," the committee predicted. The public attitude toward crime and punishment had grown increasingly enlightened over the half century, and the committee expected that "within the next decade or two the need for prisons [would] be materially reduced." [16]

What this committee could not see was that, once established, California's basic prison system proved a stable part of the state's infrastructure. At San Quentin, the first cellblock, the Stones, remained in use until 1959. At Folsom, the quarry finally closed in 1947, but a license-plate factory replaced it in 1950. At Chino, still under Kenyon Scudder's leadership, a Reception Guidance Center opened in 1951 to diagnose and classify new convicts. At Tehachapi, the California Institute for Women closed after a destructive earthquake hit in 1952, but a new women's prison opened at Corona. Changes occurred with time, but the fundamental system allowing for gradations of custody remained in place, and that system, and even those prisons, have continued to shape the perception of penal options.

Thus, instead of perceiving a reduction in the need for prisons, California has desired to expand and diversify its system further. To that end, the

state built fifteen new correctional institutions or major institutional compo-
nents between 1944 and 1974, and in 1989, the state was seeking a site near
Los Angeles for another new prison. This growth in the number of institutions highlights another of the 1954 committee's observations as, in fact,
prophetic: "Naturally," the committee wrote, "as long as the public demands
punitive imprisonment, the need for prisons cannot decrease materially." [17]

For reference, Tables 1 and 2 show, respectively, the growth in population of the state prisons at San Quentin and Folsom during the period of this study, and the number of cells in each. Comprehending the space available for each inmate, however, is not a simple matter of dividing the number of cells by the population. Not all inmates resided in cells. Many in San Quentin, for example, lived in the one large room in the "Stones." Later, many lived off the prison grounds, serving on road crews. Certainly the race of the inmate made a crucial difference in the assignment of space. The Chinese and black populations were often assigned four or more to a cell, whereas the Caucasian prisoners would usually have only a single cellmate.

The tables do show that an increasing prisoner population did not necessarily mean additional facilities.

Table 1.
Inmate populations at San Quentin and Folsom, by year

Year	San Quentin	Folsom
1855	394	——
1862	589	——
1875	883	——
1880	1,564	209
1890	1,389	662
1897	1,336	906
1910	1,915	1,016
1912	1,961	1,163
1925	3,284	1,599
1933	5,231	2,770
1937	5,088	2,808

Source: Biennial turnkey reports to the legislature;
United States Census; various prison inspection reports.
Inmate populations, of course, varied during the course of
each year.

Table 2.
Number of Cells, San Quentin and Folsom, by year

Year	San Quentin	Folsom
1855	48	——
1875	444	——
1880	696	328
1910	696	394
1920	696	394
1925	1,496	906
1936	2,500 (est.)	1,306

SOURCE: Reports of Prison Directors; reports of wardens; prison inspection reports; report to Prison Industries Reorganization Administration, 1937.

NOTES

NOTES TO THE INTRODUCTION

1. "An act providing for securing . . ." in *California Statutes*, 1851, ch. 114, p. 427; centralizing the prison system is provided for in *California Statutes*, 1944, Third Extra Session, ch. 2.

2. Many architectural historians touch on the development of prison architecture, especially when referring to significant architects. In the main, however, sociologists have paid more attention to the subject. This quotation is in Norman Johnston's, *The Human Cage: A Brief History of Prison Architecture*, p. 31. It is from the specifications of the building commissioners who hired architect John Haviland to design a solitary prison at Cherry Hill, the Eastern Penitentiary, which opened in 1829.

3. Penologists have for a while acknowledged the constraining relationship between fortress-style prison architecture and progress in their field. In 1967, for example, the President's Commission on Law Enforcement and Administration of Justice reported, "Much of today's institutional programming is circumscribed by outmoded architecture, or by prisons built with only economy, isolation, or security in mind." *Task Force Report* (Washington, D.C.: USGPO, 1967), p. 182. Penologists have also recognized the relationship between concepts of democracy and incarceration. See, for example, the 1958 article by the noted penologist Thorsten Sellin, "Corrections in Historical Perspective," p. 15: "From the point of view of penology, [democracy] meant the shift from capital and corporal punishments and torture, which were looked upon as instrumentalities of a feudal age, to punishments consisting of the deprivation of liberty and, therefore, more fitting for persons who had by their crimes forfeited their right to enjoy the privilege of freedom."

4. William H. Pierson, Jr., *American Buildings and Their Architects: the Colonial and Neo-Classical Styles*, p. 348. In subsequent prison design, Americans echoed the massiveness of Latrobe's large-cut stone entrance, but abandoned much of the interior, which provided water closets and dormitory rooms for trusted prisoners. These features and the semicircular arrangement of cells became more common in European prisons in the nineteenth century.

5. Blake McKelvey, *American Prisons: A Study in American Social History Prior to 1915* (Chicago: University of Chicago Press, 1936), p. 11.

6. The role of the Quakers in American penal and prison reform is well-documented. Blake McKelvey, ibid., provides what is probably the best survey of their activities. He revised his early work to encompass the period 1915–68 in *American Prisons: A History of Good Intentions*. The other classic survey history covering an

earlier period is Orlando F. Lewis's, *The Development of American Prisons and Prison Customs, 1776–1845, with Special Reference to Early Institutions in the State of New York.*

7. Because of the significance of Auburn in establishing the basis for prisons across America, almost all discussions of penology, previous or contemporary, contend with Lynds's system. See Lewis, *American Prisons* and McKelvey, *American Social History* and *Good Intentions,* passim; Howard B. Gill, "Correctional Philosophy and Architecture"; Johnston, *The Human Cage,* pp. 38–41; and Frederick G. Pettigrove, "The State Prisons of the United States under Separate and Congregate Systems," in *Penal and Reformatory Institutions,* ed. Charles Richmond Henderson, pp. 27–67, for example.

8. David J. Rothman, *Discovery of the Asylum: Social Order and Disorder in the New Republic.*

9. Michel Foucault, *Discipline and Punish: The Birth of the Prison.*

10. Dario Melossi and Massimo Pavarini, *The Prison and the Factory: Origins of the Penitentiary System.*

11. John A. Conley, "Revising Conceptions About the Origin of Prisons: The Importance of Economic Considerations."

12. Michael Stephen Hindus, *Prison and Plantation: Crime, Justice, and Authority in Massachusetts and South Carolina, 1767–1878.* Mark T. Carleton's thesis in *Politics and Punishment: The History of the Louisiana State Penal System* supports Hindus's interpretation, also. His study supports the contention that Louisiana developed its prison system in great part to maintain at least some blacks in servitude.

13. John Mason Jeffrey, "Discipline in the Arizona Territorial Prison: Draconian Severity or Enlightened Administration?" *Journal of Arizona History* 9, no. 3 (1968): 140–54; James A. Wilson, "Frontier in the Shadows: Prisons in the Far Southwest, 1850–1917," *Arizona and the West* 22, no. 4 (1980): 323–42; Elinor M. McGinn, "Trying to Profit: Inmate Labor at Canon City, 1872–1927," *Colorado Heritage* 2 (1987): 14–29; Gordon L. Olson, "I Felt Like I Must Be Entering . . . Another World"; Gary R. Kremer and Thomas E. Gage, "The Prison Against the Town: Jefferson City and the Penitentiary in the Nineteenth Century," *Missouri Historical Review* 74, no. 4 (1980): 414–32; Harry R. Hougen, "The Impact of Politics and Prison Industry on the General Management of the Kansas State Penitentiary," *Kansas Historical Quarterly* 43, no. 3 (1977): 297–318; and John A. Conley, "Prisons, Production, and Profit: Reconsidering the Importance of Prison Industries."

14. Annual Report of State Prison Inspectors, 1851–52, D575, GP1:138, California State Archives.

15. Warden James A. Johnson of San Quentin prison wrote the "germ of goodness" line in his report printed in the Biennial Report of the Board of Directors of the California State Prison, 1877–79.

NOTES TO CHAPTER 1

1. See, for example, George R. Stewart, *Committee of Vigilance: Revolution in San Francisco, 1851* (Boston: Houghton Mifflin Co., 1964).

2. Report to the California State Legislature on Crime and Criminals, 1851, *Appendix, Senate Journal*.

3. *California Statutes*, 1851, ch. 114, p. 427.

4. Kentucky seems to have been first to initiate such a lease system. See McKelvey, *Good Intentions*.

5. For chronologies of the highlights of the California state prisons, see Milton Chernin, "A History of California State Administration in the Field of Penology," (Master's thesis, University of California, Los Angeles, 1929); Tirey L. Ford, *California State Prisons: Their History, Development, and Management*; Lloyd L. Voigt, *History of California State Correctional Administration from 1930 to 1948*; and California Department of Corrections, *Program Analysis and Recommendations*, Program Planning Report, vol. 2, April 1978.

6. *California Statutes*, 1852, ch. 59, p. 132.

7. Chernin, "California State Administration," p. 4. Pettigrove, "State Prisons," pp. 39–40.

8. Kenneth Lamott, *Chronicles of San Quentin: The Biography of a Prison*, p. 13.; also see James H. Wilkins, "The Evolution of a State Prison," installment 2; and Clare V. McKanna, Jr., "The Origins of San Quentin, 1851–1880," *California History* 66, no. 1 (1987): 49–54, 73.

9. Testimony taken before the Select Committee on the Investigation of the Circumstances of the Passage of the State Prison Law at the Session of 1852, *Appendix, Senate Journal*, 1853, Doc. No. 34, pp. 33–34.

10. Pettigrove, "State Prisons," pp. 36–37.

11. Testimony taken before the Select Committee on the Investigation of the Circumstances of the Passage of the State Prison Law at the Session of 1852, *Appendix, Senate Journal*, 1853, Doc. No. 34, pp. 21–29.

12. Ibid., 34–35.

13. Ibid., 35–36.

14. Ibid.

15. Report of the Select Committee to Examine the State Prison, J. R. Snyder, Chairman, 1853, D64, LP2:209, California State Archives.

16. Ibid. Also, the Report of the Superintendent of State Prisons, June 28, 1855, D648, LP3:75, California State Archives, reported that since January 1851 the following convicts had been received at the state prison:

Number of Convicts	Crime
18	manslaughter
381	grand larceny
20	burglary

9	rape
1	sodomy
4	perjury
6	forgery
32	assault/intent to kill
4	mayhem
24	highway robbery
11	murder
4	abetting escape
12	assault/deadly weapon
1	arson
3	receiving stolen goods
3	assault and battery

The report also noted that only 226 of these 527 were United States citizens. These figures total 533 convicts rather than the 527 mentioned above because several prisoners were received more than once.

17. Ibid.

18. The committee members recognized the potential for conflict between prison labor and free labor, but thought it would be deflected for some time in California: "As regards the present system of prison labour, . . . it no doubt interferes with independent labour in mechanical branches, but in this State its evils have not been felt to the extent that they have been in more populous parts of our country and it is not likely that they will be for a number of years." Ibid.

19. Report of the Select Committee to Examine the State Prison, J. R. Snyder, Chairman, 1853, D64, LP2:209, California State Archives.

20. Ibid., p. 43.

21. Wilkins, "The Evolution of a State Prison," installment 5.

22. Report of the Special Committee on State Prison, March 29, 1855, *Appendix, Assembly Journal*, 1855, Doc. No. 22 contains a discussion of California's rights and obligations under the contract with Estell, concluding that it remained the state's obligation to build the prison. The "Report of the Grand Jury of Marin County" contained the assertion that "at the time the [State Prison] was so located in Marin County the citizens of said county were assured that there would not be more than fifty convicts at any one time confined in said prison." In Report of Committee Relative to the Condition and Management of the State Prison, *Appendix, Assembly Journal*, 1855, Doc. No. 26, p. 11.

23. Report of Superintendent of State Prisons, June 28, 1855, D648, LP3:75, California State Archives.

24. Ibid.

25. Ibid.; Report of Committee Relative to the Condition and Management of the State Prison, *Appendix, Assembly Journal*, 1855, Doc. No. 26, p. 6.

26. Report of Committee Relative to the Condition and Management of the State Prison, *Appendix, Assembly Journal*, 1855, Doc. No. 26, p. 7.

27. Ibid., p. 7 and Report of the Special Committee on State Prison, March 29, 1855, *Appendix, Assembly Journal*, 1855, Doc. No. 22, p. 4.

28. Report of Committee Relative to the Condition and Management of the State Prison, *Appendix, Assembly Journal*, 1855, Doc. No. 26, p. 10.

29. Ibid., p. 8.

30. Ibid., pp. 11–12.

31. Testimony of A. Jackson Tice in ibid., p. 43.

32. Ibid., passim; ibid., p. 49.

33. Ibid., p. 46.

34. Ibid., p. 10.

35. Ibid., pp. 8–10.

36. Ibid., p. 10 and Sheldon L. Messinger, John E. Berecochea, David Rauma, and Richard A. Berk, "The Foundations of Parole in California."

37. Ibid., p. 46.

38. *California Statutes*, 1855, ch. 224, p. 292; Report on State Prison by Joint Committee of Senate and Assembly, *Appendix, Assembly Journal*, 1856, p. 3.

39. Report on State Prison by Joint Committee of Senate and Assembly, *Appendix, Assembly Journal*, 1856, pp. 35–36.

40. Ibid., Appendix K.

41. *California Statutes*, 1856, ch. 39, p. 48.

42. Ibid. and Report of Committee on State Prison submitted February 25, 1857, *Appendix, Assembly Journal*, 1858, 8th Sess. See also the colorful account in Lamott, *Chronicles of San Quentin*.

43. Report of Committee on State Prison submitted February 25, 1857, *Appendix, Assembly Journal*, 1858, 8th Sess.

44. Harold Kirker, *California's Architectural Frontier: Style and Tradition in the Nineteenth Century*, p. 74, and Kirker's files, Department of History, University of California, Santa Barbara; Report of Committee on State Prison submitted February 25, 1857, *Appendix, Assembly Journal*, 1858, 8th Sess.

45. San Quentin Miscellany, 1855–58, D815, F3617:275, California State Archives.

46. Report of the Joint Committee Investigation Regarding General Affairs and Conditions at State Prison, 1858, California State Archives.

47. Ibid.

48. Ibid.

49. Report of the Investigation Regarding Conditions at San Quentin State Prison, April 16, 1859, Dr650:LP4, 1859–61, California State Archives.

50. *California Statutes*, 1858, ch. 43, p. 32, and the *State of California* v. *John F. McCauley and Lloyd Tevis*, Seventh Judicial District, County of Marin, State of California, 1859–1860, Dr650, LP4, California State Archives.

51. Report of the Board of Directors of the California State Prison, December 31, 1860.

52. Report on State Prison Conditions, April 5, 1862, Dr651:LP5, California State Archives.

53. Ibid. In 1859, attorneys for prison sublessee John F. McCauley and for the estate of James M. Estell, offered an alternate cause-and-effect analysis of the relationship between the legal dispute with the state and the high rate of escape: Point 23 noted that a "state of disaffection" existed among the convicts because the government's contest of the lease led them to believe they were "unlawfully held in custody." See the Crockett and Crittenden brief among the legal papers of Gregory Yale, C-B, 461, the Bancroft Library, University of California, Berkeley.

54. Biennial Report of Directors of California State Prison, 1865–67. Prison population data supplied by Richard Berk, Department of Sociology, University of California, Santa Barbara.

55. *Seventh Annual Report of the California Prison Commission for the Year 1871–72* (San Francisco: Jos. Winterburn & Co., 1871), p. 30.

56. Report of the Joint Committee Investigation Regarding General Affairs and Conditions at State Prison, 1858, California State Archives.

57. *Fifth Annual Report of the California Prison Commission for the Year 1869–70* (San Francisco: Jos. Winterburn & Co., 1871).

NOTES TO CHAPTER 2

1. McKelvey, *American Social History*, pp. 76–77. Sheldon Messinger, Richard A. Berk, and colleagues have been collecting and studying California's historic prison population data in order to test hypotheses relating incarceration rates to other social, economic, and legal phenomena, and they kindly supplied the author with a variety of census data. They show that the population of males aged 15 to 29 years in California in 1860 was 102,688. In 1865, it was only 96,839. The corresponding data for women were 35,295 and 44,187. Messinger and Berk have published a number of papers in which they discuss their findings. See, for example, Berk, David Rauma, Sheldon Messinger, and Thomas F. Cooley, "A Test of the Stability of Punishment Hypothesis: The Case of California, 1851–1970," pp. 805–29.

2. *California Statutes*, 1858, ch. 354, p. 339.

3. See descriptions in Report of the Joint Committee Investigation Regarding General Affairs and Conditions at State Prison, 1858, California State Archives.

4. Minority Report of the Directors of the State Prison to the Legislature of the State of California, submitted February 16, 1856, *Appendix, Assembly Journal*, 1856, Doc. No. 11., p. 9.

5. Ibid., p. 11.

6. Report on State Prison by Joint Committee of Senate and Assembly, *Appendix, Assembly Journal*, 1856, pp. 35–36.

7. Report of the Joint Committee Investigation Regarding General Affairs and Conditions at State Prison, 1858, California State Archives; *California Statutes*, 1858, ch. 354, p. 339, Sec. 6.

8. Report of the Investigation Regarding Conditions at San Quentin State Prison, April 16, 1859, Dr650:LP4, 1859–61, California State Archives.

9. Ibid. and Report of the Joint Committee Investigation Regarding General Affairs and Conditions at State Prison, 1858, California State Archives.

10. For a detailed history of the state's struggle to control prison administration, see Chernin, "California State Administration."

11. *California Statutes*, 1868, ch. 468, p. 627.

12. Report of the Joint State Prison Committee on the Construction of the Branch Prison at Folsom, March 1880.

13. *First Annual Report of the California Prison Commission* (San Francisco: Towne and Bacon, 1867), p. 4. For a complete set of the thirty-seven Articles, see Charles Richmond Henderson, ed. *Prison Reform: Correction and Prevention*, pp. 39–63.

14. See ibid. for exposition of these principles. Also see, Enoch Cobb Wines and Theodore Dwight, *Report on the Prisons and Reformatories of the United States and Canada, Made to the Legislature of New York, January, 1867*, and Torsten Eriksson, *The Reformers: An Historical Survey of Pioneer Experiments in the Treatment of Criminals*, pp. 81–88.

15. *Seventh Annual Report of the California Prison Commission for the Year 1871–72*, pp. 27–31.

16. Ibid., pp. 27–31.

17. Report of the Joint State Prison Committee on the Construction of the Branch Prison at Folsom, March 1880, pp. 5–6.

18. Ibid., p. 7.

19. Hubert H. Bancroft, "History of California, vol. 7, 1860–1890," in *The Works of Hubert Howe Bancroft* (1890; reprint, Santa Barbara: Wallace Hebberd, 1970), p. 367, note; Report of the Joint State Prison Committee on the Construction of the Branch Prison at Folsom, March 1880.

20. Report of the Joint State Prison Committee on the Construction of the Branch Prison at Folsom, March 1880.

21. Ibid., p. 7.

22. Ibid., p. 9.

23. Answers to Committee's Questions, State Prison at Folsom, 1897–98, D655, LP9:4, California State Archives.

24. Report of the Joint State Prison Committee on the Construction of the Branch Prison at Folsom, March 1880, pp. 9–12.

25. Report of the Joint State Prison Committee as to the Management of the Prison at San Quentin and the Construction of the Branch Prison at Folsom, 1880; *California Statutes*, 1880, ch. 50, p. 39; and *California Statutes*, 1881, ch. 38, p. 33.

26. Report of Warden, State Prison at Folsom, November 1, 1880, in First Annual Report of State Board of Prison Directors.

27. Report of Clerk, State Prison at Folsom, November 1, 1880, in First Annual Report of State Board of Prison Directors.

28. Report of Warden, State Prison at Folsom, November 1, 1880, in First Annual Report of State Board of Prison Directors.

29. Michael D. Brown, *History of Folsom Prison*; *California Statutes*, 1883, ch. 71, p. 295; and Answers to Committee's Questions, State Prison at Folsom, 1897–98, D655, LP9:4, California State Archives.

30. Reprinted in Henderson, *Prison Reform*, p. 39.

31. *Seventh Annual Report of the California Prison Commission for the Year 1871–72.*

32. Report on State Prison Conditions, 1875, bin 217, California State Archives; *California Statutes*, 1876, ch. 552, p. 832.

33. See, for example, nineteenth-century pamphlets by California authors, "The Convict Labor Question in California," F862, P19, x, Bancroft Library, University of California, Berkeley.

34. Report on State Prison Conditions, 1875, bin 217, California State Archives.

35. See Biennial Report of the Board of Directors of the California State Prison, 1877–79, p. 17.

36. See, for example, commentary on the labor changes in the First Annual Report of the State Board of Prison Directors, 1880, pp. 6–7.

37. See, for example, *San Francisco Chronicle*, 1879, passim.

38. *California Statutes*, 1880, ch. 71, p. 67; Enoch Cobb Wines, *The State of Prisons and Child-Saving Institutions in the Civilized World* (1880; reprint, Montclair, N.Y.: Patterson Smith, 1968).

39. Report of the Assembly Committee on State Prisons, 1881, p. 3.

40. Report of the Senate Committee on State Prisons and Prison Buildings, 1883.

41. Ibid.

42. Biennial Report of the Folsom State Prison, *Appendix, Senate Journal*, 1895, vol. 6.

43. See, for example, "Labor of Convicts, The Stonecutters hold a mass-meeting," *San Francisco Chronicle*, July 24, 1887.

44. *San Francisco Chronicle*, July 2, 1887 through Aug. 14, 1887, passim. Quotations about Schmidt are from "Iron Bracelets," *San Francisco Chronicle*, Aug. 14, 1887.

45. Brown, *History of Folsom Prison*, ch. 3.

46. *California Statutes*, 1889, ch. 103, p. 100 (Preston); ibid., 1889, ch. 108, p. 111 (Whittier).

47. For example, Lawrence M. Friedman, "Plea Bargaining in Historical Perspective."

48. *California Statutes*, 1864, ch. 324, p. 356.

49. Sheldon L. Messinger, et al., "The Foundations of Parole in California."

50. Ibid.

51. *California Statutes*, 1889, ch. 103, p. 100; ibid., ch. 108, p. 111.

52. *California Statutes*, 1893, ch. 153, p. 183.

53. Report of Special Assembly Committee on State Prison Reform, *Assembly Journal*, 1907, p. 274.

54. Answers to Committee's Questions, State Prison at Folsom, 1897–98, D655, LP9:4, California State Archives.

55. Report of the State Board of Prison Directors, 1895.

56. Senate Bill 738, *Senate Journal*, 1895.

57. Answers to Committee's Questions, State Prison at Folsom, 1897–98, D655, LP9:4, California State Archives.

58. *Annual Report* of the California Prison Commission, March 1902; Brown, *History of Folsom Prison*.

59. Proceedings of Senate and Assembly Relative to California State Prisons, *Assembly Journal*, 1903; *San Francisco Examiner*, July 29, 1903; and Jack Black, *The Big Break at Folsom: A Story of the Revolt of Prison Tyranny*.

60. *San Francisco Examiner*, July 29, 1903; Jack Black, *The Big Break at Folsom*.

61. Report of State Board of Prison Directors, August 22, 1903.

62. Jack Black, "The Big Break at Folsom: A Story of the Revolt of Prison Tyranny by Jack Black with a Sequel by the Same Author, Out of Prison," n. d., California State Library, Sacramento, p. 27.

63. Report of State Board of Prison Directors, August 22, 1903, and Proceedings of Senate and Assembly Relative to California State Prisons, *Assembly Journal*, 1903, p. 19.

64. Warden's Report, in Board of Prison Directors Report, 1905, in Second Biennial Report of the State Board of Charities and Corrections, 1906.

65. Warden's Report, in Board of Prison Directors Report, 1907, in Third Biennial Report of the State Board of Charities and Corrections, 1908; Warden's Report, in Board of Prison Directors Report, 1909, in Fourth Biennial Report of the State Board of Charities and Corrections, 1910; and *California Statutes*, 1921, ch. 394, p. 579, allocated funds, finally, for completion of the wall.

66. Report of Special Assembly Committee on State Prison Reform, *Assembly Journal*, 1907, p. 274.

67. Ford, *California State Prisons*; *Assembly Journal*, 1905, p. 1404; *California Statutes*, 1911, ch. 56, p. 71; and State Board of Prison Directors Report, 1912, cited in Chernin, "California State Administration," p. 124.

68. *California Statutes*, 1917, ch. 534, p. 688.

NOTES TO CHAPTER 3

1. The San Quentin census stood at 1,451 men and 27 women in 1904, whereas the Folsom population stood at 927. See First Biennial Report of the State Board of Charities and Corrections, 1903–1904, p. 11.

2. Report of the State Board of Prison Directors of the State of California upon a Proposed Reformatory for Adult Offenders, December 1910, Exhibit B.

3. *California Statutes*, 1903, ch. 371, p. 519.

4. In 1945, the legislature finally appropriated adequate funds for such an institution in Vacaville. See Voight, *California State Correctional Administration*.

5. *California Statutes*, 1903, ch. 363, p. 482.

6. Second Biennial Report of the State Board of Charities and Corrections, 1904–1906, p. 7. In addition to the two prisons, these included the two reform schools, five hospitals for the insane, one home for the deaf, the blind, and one for the "feeble-minded," as well as county and city jails and county almshouses.

7. *California Statutes*, 1903, ch. 34, p. 34, and ibid., ch. 35, p. 36. The legislators finally agreed to pay probation officers in 1917. Ibid., ch. 732, p. 1409.

8. *California Statutes*, 1864, ch. 324, p. 356; ibid., 1880, ch. 71, p. 67.

9. Ford, *California State Prisons*, pp. 60–69, and Griffith J. Griffith, "Legislation in Behalf of Prisons: California Far Behind Other States in Up-to-Date Methods," *Sacramento Bee*, Mar. 5, 1907; *California Statutes*, 1901, ch. 64, p. 82.

10. For a still-valuable summary of these statutory reforms, see Chernin, "California State Administration," pp. 140–45.

11. San Quentin Register, California State Archives; J. Wess Moore, *Glimpse of Prison Life*, p. 3.

12. San Quentin Register, California State Archives.

13. Moore, *Glimpse of Prison Life*, p. 14.

14. Ibid. This quote is from a reprint of a piece Moore wrote while in San Quentin.

15. Ibid. and San Quentin Minute Book, California State Archives.

16. Proceedings of Senate and Assembly Relative to California State Prisons, *Assembly Journal*, 1903, p. 15.

17. Ibid., pp. 15–16.

18. Ibid., passim.

19. Ibid., minority report; First Biennial Report of the State Board of Charities and Corrections, 1904–1906, p. 20.

20. *Annual Reports* of the California Prison Commission, various years; Mary Alderman Garbutt, *Victories of Four Decades: A History of the Woman's Christian Temperance Union of Southern California, 1883–1924*; and Commonwealth Club of California, *Transactions*, various numbers.

21. Pardee Scrapbook 55, Bancroft Library, University of California, Berkeley.

22. Pardee Scrapbook 11, Bancroft Library, University of California, Berkeley.

23. Accounts of Tompkins's various affronts may be found in numerous northern California newspapers from 1904 through 1906. The Pardee scrapbooks, housed in the Bancroft Library, University of California, Berkeley, contain a concentrated collection of relevant clippings from newspapers such as the *Fresno Republican*, the *Napa Register*, the *Sacramento Bee*, the *San Francisco Bulletin*, the *San Francisco Call*, the *San Francisco Chronicle*, the *San Francisco Examiner*, and the *San Jose Herald*. For the description of Hoyle as warden, see California Department of Corrections, *Program Analysis and Recommendations*, Program Planning Report, vol. 2, Appendix A, p. 4.

24. Moore, *Glimpse of Prison Life*, p. 3.

25. See Correspondence, California State Prison Commission, Archives, California State Library, California Room.

26. In a letter from State Prison Commissioner Chair's secretary, Carrere, to J. Wess Moore, the following question was asked:

"3. You say that if there is any credit due for the making of it possible for your association of life-sentenced prisoners to begin your work, it is due Warden Tompkins, Captain Harrison, and other officials of the prison.

State how it came about that you formed such an association and in what manner you were assisted and by what officers."
Moore's response, unfortunately, is not extant.

For Tompkins's punishment of Moore and support by Drahms, see Moore, *Glimpse of Prison Life*, pp. 1–2 and 4. For the press release and the *Los Angeles Times* editorial, see Pardee Scrapbook 11, Bancroft Library, University of California, Berkeley.

27. Second Biennial Report of the State Board of Charities and Corrections, 1904–1906, p. 27; Correspondence, California State Prison Commission, Archives, California State Library, California Room.

28. Correspondence, California State Prison Commission, Archives, California State Library, California Room.

29. Ibid., dated 1906.

30. *Men of California, 1901*, p. 402, in California State Library, and see articles in *San Francisco Call* for Sept. 3, 5–10, and 29 and Oct. 11, 14, 22, and 24, 1903, and *San Francisco Chronicle*, Mar. 4, 11, and 24, 1904, and Mar. 2 and 30, 1905.

31. Griffith J. Griffith, "The Autobiography of Griffith Jenkins Griffith," n.d., in Special Collections, University of California, Los Angeles.

32. "Supreme Court Decision Against Griffith J. Griffith," *San Francisco Chronicle*, Mar. 30, 1905; Colonel Griffith's Christmas letter to only child, from San Quentin Prison, December 20, 1905, Special Collections, University of California, Los Angeles.

33. "Criticises Prison Board," *Sacramento Bee*, Feb. 19, 1907.

34. Biennial Report of the State Board of Prison Directors, *Appendix, Senate Journal*, 1907; "Criticises Prison Board," *Sacramento Bee*, Feb. 19, 1907.

35. See Garbutt, *Victories of Four Decades*; California State Board of Prison Directors, *Rules and Regulations for the Paroling of Prisoners*; and Ford, *California State Prisons*.

36. See Chernin, "California State Administration," for a recount of post-Tompkins reforms.

37. *San Francisco Daily News*, June 5, 1909, and San Quentin Register, California State Archives.

38. Griffith J. Griffith, "Legislation in Behalf of Prisons," *Sacramento Bee*, Mar. 5, 1907; and *California Statutes*, 1917, ch. 527, p. 270.

39. See, for example, the *San Francisco Chronicle*, Jan. 27 and 28, 1908 and Aug. 8 and 9, 1909; Prison Reform League, *Crimes and Criminals*, p. 312.

40. *Los Angeles Herald*, Dec. 31, 1910, p. 12.

41. *San Francisco Chronicle*, Dec. 12, 1912.

42. For an example of a letter from a grateful inmate, see "Words of Praise for Colonel Griffith," *Los Angeles Herald*, Apr. 4, 1907.

NOTES TO CHAPTER 4

1. "An Act Providing for Securing the State Prison Convicts," *California Statutes*, 1851, ch. 114, p. 427.

2. "Documents Connected with the State Prison," *Senate Journal*, 1853, Doc. No. 7.

3. California prison population statistics from 1851 on have been compiled and provided by Professors Richard Berk and Sheldon Messinger of the University of California. Chapter 1, sup., details the Estell scandal.

4. Report of Committee Relative to the Condition and Management of the State Prison, *Appendix, Assembly Journal*, 1855, Doc. No. 26. See especially the deposition of former guard Wm. H. White, p. 20 and State Prison engineer Thomas Young, pp. 22–24.

5. Report of the Joint Committee Investigation Regarding General Affairs and Conditions at the State Prison, 1858, California State Archives; letter from M. F. Butler to Board of State Prison Commissioners, Dec. 29, 1857, San Quentin miscellaneous correspondence, D815, F3617:275, California State Archives; and brief filed in Marin County for McCauley, c. 1859, Bancroft Library, University of California, Berkeley.

6. For one publication of San Quentin population figures, see Berk, et al., "Punishment Hypothesis." California Department of Corrections, *Program Analysis and Recommendations*, Program Planning Report, vol. 2, Appendix A. According to this official chronology, a total of five women were received at Folsom, the last one in 1929, but only the first finished her sentence there.

7. A good case in point is the Biennial Report of the Board of Directors of the California State Prison, 1877–79, which seems to cover issues from appropriate prison industries to the New Penology, but comes closest to mentioning women in Table IX, Occupation of Prisoners When Received, which lists six seamstresses.

8. Penal Institutions: State Prisons and Reformatories: State Prison at San Quentin, 1897–98, D655, LP9:4, California State Archives.

9. See Wilkins, "The Evolution of a State Prison," and Anne Louise Carter, "History and Treatment of Women in the Penal Institutions of California," (Master's thesis, University of California [Berkeley], 1949), p. 39; see *Annual Reports* of the California Prison Commission, vols. 1–9, housed, among other places, at the University of California, Berkeley; for a full discussion of the New Penology, see chapter 2; and Wines and Dwight, *Prisons and Reformatories*, pp. 69–70.

10. This article is quoted in Carter, "History and Treatment of Women"; the quotation is from p. 42.

11. Estelle B. Freedman, *Their Sisters' Keepers*. Freedman argues that upright

women needed to discover a stronger bond with fallen women than with upright men before becoming champions of female convicts. This happened as the Victorian age increasingly developed two separate spheres of life: male and female. Once the women recognized their common spheres, they sought to remove control over female prisoners from the men completely, resulting in a national reform movement for separate women's prisons governed by women.

Richard Morales, who had read Freedman's 1974 article with the same title as her book, argued similar points, although the focus of his dissertation is the difficulties faced by the founders of California's women's prison in achieving their reform goals. "History of the California Institution for Women, 1927–1960: A Woman's Regime," (Ph.D. diss., University of California, Riverside, 1980). See Edna Walker Chandler's *Women in Prison* (Indianapolis: Bobbs Merrill Co., 1973), p. 111 for a comparative chart of women's prisons.

12. See San Quentin Prison Registers, California State Archives. The attitude that women were responsible for the deeds of their criminal husbands persisted well into the first years of the California Institution for Women at Tehachapi. See transcript, "In the Matter of a Visit of the Committee to the California Institution for Women at Tehachapi," Legislative Committee on Penal Institutions Hearing, June 15, 1942, D702, LP56:33, California State Archives. See also Minutes of the Board of Trustees, California Institute for Women, Nov. 22, 1929 through 1939, typescript, passim, California Department of Corrections.

13. Henderson, *Prison Reform*, p. 45; *California Statutes*, 1903, ch. 363, p. 482; quoted in Garbutt, *Victories of Four Decades*, p. 99; see chapter 3 for details of Tompkins's reign and the resulting scandal; and Prison Reform League, *Crime and Criminals*.

14. Berk, et al., "Punishment Hypothesis."

15. Prison Reform League, *Crime and Criminals*, p. 98.

16. Ibid.

17. Ibid., p. 99.

18. Biennial Report of the State Board of Prison Directors, *Appendix, Senate Journal*, 1907, vol. 2, p. 14.

19. Clippings, Pardee Scrapbook no. 55, Bancroft Library, University of California, Berkeley.

20. Garbutt, *Victories of Four Decades*, p. 99; Freedman, *Their Sisters' Keepers*, contains a good discussion of how Progressive-era environmental determinism empowered clubwomen to act on behalf of their less fortunate sisters.

21. Biennial Report of the State Board of Prison Directors, *Appendix, Senate Journal*, 1913, vol. 2.

22. Freedman, *Their Sisters' Keepers*, p. 52.

23. Isabel C. Barrows, "Reformatory Treatment of Women in the United States," in Henderson, *Prison Reform*, p. 138–62, Freedman, *Their Sisters' Keepers*, especially ch. 4.

24. *California Statutes*, 1919, ch. 165, p. 246; *Appendix, Assembly Journal*, 1919, p. 67.

25. Hester T. Griffith, "Legislative Notes," *Southern California White Ribbon*, Mar. 1919, p. 1, available at the Los Angeles headquarters of the WCTU.

26. "Women Assist Plan for Home," *San Francisco Chronicle* Mar. 28, 1919.

27. Ibid.; "Women's Home Gets Support," *San Francisco Chronicle* Apr. 10, 1919; Dr. Ethel M. Watters, "Women in California," *Southern California White Ribbon*, May 1919.

28. *California Statutes*, 1919, ch. 165, p. 246, Sec. 36; ibid. and Report of the Department of State Institutions, 1923–24, *Appendix, Senate Journal*, 1925.

29. "Pending Legislation of 1923," *Transactions of the Commonwealth Club of California* 18, no. 2 (March 1923): 84–87.

30. For the closing of Sonoma, see Ninth Biennial Report of the State Board of Charities and Corrections, 1918–20, *Appendix, Senate Journal*, 1923, p. 39; *California Statutes*, 1919, ch. 165, p. 246, Sects. 3 and 7.

31. Garbutt, *Victories of Four Decades*, pp. 39–40; P. Evelyn Rosencrantz, "To Miss Jackson," *San Quentin Bulletin* 19, no. 6 (January 1931): 29; Lillian Christie, "And I Learned About Women From These," *San Quentin Bulletin* 17, no. 7, (February 1929): 4.

32. Ninth Biennial Report of the State Board of Charities and Corrections, 1918–20, *Appendix, Senate Journal*, 1923, p. 39.

33. *Appendix, Senate and Assembly Journals*, 1923.

34. "Clubwomen Participate in Ground Breaking at San Quentin Prison," *San Quentin Bulletin* 13, no. 2 (November 1925): 11.

35. "Transformation and Progress," *San Quentin Bulletin* 12, no. 4 (January 1926): 14–15.

36. "Work in the Women's Department," *San Quentin Bulletin* 19, no. 6 (January 1931): 29.

37. Roberta Hall, "The Open Door," *San Quentin Bulletin* 20, nos. 11 and 12 (June and July 1932): 17 and 31; Harriet Dale, "Education in Queen's House," *San Quentin Bulletin* 21, nos. 9 and 10 (April and May 1933): 27.

38. *California Statutes*, 1927, ch. 456, p. 783.

39. See, for example, Stanley's memoirs. Leo L. Stanley, *Men At Their Worst*, especially the first two chapters.

40. Ibid., p. 266; Ralph Thatcher, "A New Hospital After Fifty Years," *San Quentin Bulletin* 22, nos. 6 and 7 (January and February 1934): 10–11.

41. *California Statutes*, 1929, ch. 248, p. 490; ibid., 1927, ch. 456, p. 783; and Eleanor Miller, *When Memory Calls*, p. 193.

42. "Woman Prison Site Obtained by Trustees," *Los Angeles Times*, July 5, 1930.

43. *Senate Journal*, May 5, 1931, p. 3.

44. "Selection of Site for Women's Prison Approved by Senators," *Sausilito News*, May 29, 1931; "Broke Ground for Institution Thursday, Eighteenth," *Tehachapi News*, June 19, 1931.

45. Unattributed article, "Will Break Ground for Institution in September," c. 1930, from Scrapbook, D919 F3812, California State Archives.

46. Clipping, Emily B. Latham, "The Site of the Women's Prison at Tehachapi," *Municipal League Bulletin*, Oct. 20, 1934, California State Archives, and Emily Latham, "What Women Are Thinking: An Excursion into Penology," *San Francisco Chronicle*, Apr. 1934.

47. Latham, "The Site of the Women's Prison at Tehachapi."

48. See, for example, *San Francisco Chronicle*, July 9, 1932.

49. Biennial Report of the State Board of Prison Directors, 1931–32, p. 46; *Senate Journal*, 1933, p. 507; and *California Statutes*, 1933, ch. 102, p. 557.

50. For a description of the fence, see Carter, "History and Treatment of Women," p. 96; Stanley, *Men At Their Worst*, p. 267.

51. Margot Royal, "On the Trail of the Rainbow," *San Quentin Bulletin* 22, no. 4 (Nov. 1933): 8; "In the Matter of a Visit of the Committee to the California Institution for Women at Tehachapi," Legislative Committee on Penal Institutions Hearing, June 15, 1942, D702, LP56:33, California State Archives.

52. "California Helps Women Get Back on Straight Road," *Christian Science Monitor*, Nov. 28, 1933; "Feminists Hail Appointment of Woman Warden at Tehachapi," *San Francisco Chronicle*, Mar. 9, 1934; and unattributed column by Harry Carr, n.d., Tehachapi scrapbook, D919, F3812:1–2, California State Archives.

53. "Feminists Hail Appointment," *San Francisco Chronicle*, Mar. 9, 1934.

54. Ibid.; "Woman Made Deputy Warden for Tehachapi," *San Francisco Chronicle*, Mar. 7, 1934.

55. Clipping, Ethel Bogardus, "Let Women Manage Tehachapi and It Will Be Success," *San Francisco Chronicle*, n.d., Tehachapi scrapbook, California State Archives.

56. "Separate Women's Prison Gets Backing of Merriam," *San Francisco Chronicle*, Oct. 14, 1934.

57. Letter, Mrs. James Pope to Mrs. Paul Eliel, Jan. 22, 1934, League of Women Voters Collection, Urban Archives, California State University, Northridge; Letter, Mrs. Everett Latham to Mrs. Paul Eliel, Feb. 2, 1934, ibid.

58. *California Statutes*, 1935, ch. 497, p. 566; See advertisement, "Vote Yes on Senate Constitutional Amendment," League of Women Voters Collection, Urban Archives, California State University, Northridge.

59. Advertisement, "Vote Yes on Senate Constitutional Amendment," ibid.

60. Unattributed clipping, "Board Named for Prison," n.d., Tehachapi scrapbook, California State Archives.

61. Unattributed clipping, "Proposed Women's Prison Board," Oct. 12, 1935, Tehachapi scrapbook, California State Archives.

NOTES TO CHAPTER 5

1. *First Annual Report of the California Prison Commission*; see, for example, Report on State Prison Conditions, April 5, 1862, Dr651:LP5, California State Archives,

which calls for a new building to allow for classification and segregation of prisoners; and *California Statutes*, 1911, ch. 570, p. 1088.

2. *Fifth Annual Report of the California Prison Commission for the Year 1869–70*, pp. 39–40.

3. *Seventh Annual Report of the California Prison Commission for the Year 1871–72*, pp. 27–29.

4. Report of the Joint Committee Investigation Regarding General Affairs and Conditions at State Prison, 1858, California State Archives. This report recommended moving the prison to a better location "with a quantity of granite."

5. See, for example, Biennial Report of the Board of Directors of the California State Prison, 1871–73, p. 8, in which R. Pacheco, warden of San Quentin calls for immediate construction of five hundred new cells.

6. E. R. Highton, *Observations on the Qualifications and Professional Training of Officers for Prisons and Reformatories*.

7. Biennial Report of State Board of Prison Directors, 1893–94, p. 7.

8. Proceedings of Senate and Assembly Relative to California State Prisons, *Assembly Journal*, 1903, p. 19; First Biennial Report of the State Board of Charities and Corrections, 1903–1904, p. 15; and *California Statutes*, 1917, ch. 534, p. 688.

9. For more details of the scandals publicized in 1904–1905, see chapter 4, sup. That the legislature knew about standards for East Coast prisons and cared about being inferior can be gleaned from many official reports. One clear example is the Report of Select Committee on State Prisons and Reformatory Institutions, March 10, 1903, p. 15, where the Assembly resolved that "California boasts its place in the front rank of States, but her prisons lag a generation behind the better class of Eastern penitentiaries," in Ford, *California State Prisons*, p. 56; *California Statutes*, 1909, ch. 553, p. 876.

10. Report of the State Board of Prison Directors of the State of California upon a Proposed Reformatory for Adult Offenders, December 1910; *California Statutes*, 1911, ch. 570, p. 1088.

11. *California Statutes*, 1917, ch. 534, p. 688; ibid., 1921, ch. 615, p. 1051.

12. Ibid., 1927, ch. 45, p. 2302; ibid., 1929, ch. 59, p. 2232.

13. Ibid., 1929, ch. 684, p. 1176, created the young men's reformatory.

14. Ibid., ch. 191, p. 350.

15. Ibid., ch. 248, p. 490; see, for example, C. A. Jones, "Inquiry Begun on Prison Site," *Los Angeles Times*, Apr. 24, 1931.

16. Warren H. Atherton, "Prisons, Prisoners, and Paroles: A Problem in Penology," typewritten speech to the Commonwealth Club, c. 1934, California State Library, California Room, and Frank C. Sykes, "Prisons and Paroles," typewritten speech, c. 1934, ibid.

17. Ethel Bogardis, "Let Women Manage Tehachapi and It Will Be Success," *San Francisco Chronicle*, c. 1934; "Separate Women's Prison Gets Backing of Merriam," *San Francisco Chronicle*, Oct. 14, 1934; and editorial in *Tehachapi News*, Oct. 19, 1934.

18. *California Statutes*, 1935, ch. 414, p. 1465.

19. Ibid.

20. Documented in Report of Joint Legislative Fact-Finding Committee on the Southern California Prison at Chino, March 5, 1941, p. 17.

21. *California Statutes*, 1937, ch. 378, p. 1195.

22. Report of Joint Legislative Fact-Finding Committee on Southern California Prison at Chino, March 5, 1941, p. 51.

23. Ibid., p. 58, 57, and 50.

24. Ibid., p. 19.

25. Ibid., p. 55.

26. "San Quentin Prisoners Start Hunger Strike to Get More Meat," *San Francisco Chronicle*, Mar. 21, 1939; *California Statutes*, 1939, ch. 55, p. 479.

27. See "Supplemental Charges and Specification of Charges" and other relevant hearing and decision documents, Dr. 1406, F3450, California State Archives.

28. Clinton T. Duffy, as told to Dean Jennings, *The San Quentin Story*, pp. 23–56; "Court Smith is New San Quentin Warden," *San Quentin Bulletin*, March–April 1936, p. 22.

29. Duffy, *The San Quentin Story*, p. 59; "Opinion of the Governor," pp. 26–27, Dr. 1406, F3450, California State Archives.

30. "Opinion of the Governor," pp. 5–14, Dr. 1406, F3450, California State Archives.

31. "Argument on Behalf of the Respondents," pp. 2808 and 2809, Dr. 1406, F3450, California State Archives.

32. *California Statutes*, 1941, Constitution of 1879, as amended, Art. X, Sec. 3, p. liv.

33. "New State Prison Board Begins Action for Reform," *Los Angeles Times*, July 13, 1940.

34. Duffy, *The San Quentin Story*, pp. 60–80, and "Smith Resigns as Warden of San Quentin," *Los Angeles Times*, July 14, 1940.

35. Kenyon J. Scudder, *Prisoners Are People*, pp. 18–19.

36. Ibid., p. 21.

37. "Selecting Our Staff Personnel," ibid., pp. 30–43.

38. See description in Report of Joint Legislative Fact-Finding Committee on the Southern California Prison at Chino, March 5, 1941, passim.

39. Ibid., p. 100.

40. Scudder, *Prisoners Are People*, pp. 22–29; Report of Joint Legislative Fact-Finding Committee on the Southern California Prison at Chino, March 5, 1941, and Biennial Report of State Board of Prison Directors, 1939–41.

41. Scudder, *Prisoners Are People*, p. 51, and Kenyon J. Scudder, *Between Dark and Daylight*.

42. *California Statutes*, 1941, ch. 1192, p. 2963; Final Report of Governor's Investigation Committee on Penal Affairs, January 21, 1944, pp. 32–34.

43. "First Chino Inmates Due," *Los Angeles Times*, July 10, 1941, and Scudder, *Prisoners Are People*, pp. 44–52.

44. Final Report of Governor's Investigation Committee on Penal Affairs, January 21, 1944, and Scudder, *Prisoners Are People*, p. 47.

45. Scudder, *Prisoners Are People*, p. 47.

NOTES TO CHAPTER 6

1. For the story of the effect of the New Deal on California government, see Robert E. Burke, *Olson's New Deal for California*, and James T. Patterson, *The New Deal and the States: Federalism in Transition*; for radical politics in California during the depression, see Arthur M. Schlesinger, Jr., *The Politics of Upheaval*.

2. Report of Joint Legislative Fact-Finding Committee on the Southern California Prison at Chino, March 5, 1941, p. 10.

3. *California Statutes*, 1941, Constitution of 1879, as amended, Art. X, Sec. 7, p. liv.

4. Many of the details of Warren's moves and motives come from an interview with Richard A. McGee, taped on an unrecorded date in January 1982, at the American Justice Institute (AJI) in Sacramento, conducted by the author and in the author's files. McGee was Warren's choice to be the first professional director of corrections, and he retained that post for over twenty-three years, until his retirement, when he started the AJI think tank.

For substantiation of the furor, a perusal of the *San Francisco Chronicle* from Nov. 26, 1943, through Jan. 31, 1944, uncovered close to seventy articles about Sampsell and the subsequent investigation.

5. *San Francisco Chronicle*, Nov. 26, 1943 to Jan. 31, 1944, passim, and Final Report of Governor's Investigation Committee on Penal Affairs, January 21, 1944.

6. McGee interview, Jan. 1982.

7. Final Report of Governor's Investigation Committee on Penal Affairs, January 21, 1944, pp. 37–39.

8. "Warren May Agree to Head Delegation," *San Francisco Chronicle*, Jan. 8, 1944.

9. *California Statutes*, 1944, Third Extra Session, ch. 2, p. 13.

10. "Warren Plan Opposition: Prison Reorganization Will Be Fought," *San Francisco Chronicle*, Jan. 28, 1944.

11. Earl C. Behrens, "Warren Prison Plan Stirs Up Controversy," *San Francisco Chronicle*, Jan. 28, 1944.

12. Ibid.; "Prison Bill Passes With Amendments," *San Francisco Chronicle*, Jan. 1, 1944.

13. "Prison Bill Passes," *San Francisco Chronicle*, Jan. 1, 1944, and Voigt, *California State Correctional Administration*, pp. 14–15.

14. Final Report of Governor's Investigation Committee on Penal Affairs, January 21, 1944, p. 38.

15. *California Statutes*, 1945, ch. 75, p. 385. For the building of Soledad, see Voigt, *California State Correctional Administration*.

16. Study on Building Needs of State Correctional Institutions, Partial Report of the Senate Special Committee on Governmental Administration, Released September 28, 1954, p. 30.

17. Ibid.

SELECTED BIBLIOGRAPHY

ARCHIVES

Bancroft Library, University of California, Berkeley
  Manuscripts; Miscellany; Official Reports; Oral History Tapes, Pardee Scrapbooks; Personal Collections
California State Archives, Sacramento
  Correspondence Files, Official Reports, Pardon Books, plans and photographs, Prison Clipping Files, Prison Registers, Statute Books
California State Library, Sacramento
  Information files, photographs, Prisoners' publications, California Room Clipping Files
Commonwealth Club, San Francisco
  Minutes and miscellany
Special Collections, University of California, Los Angeles
  Griffith collection, including clippings, letters, memorabilia, and publications
Urban Archives, California State University, Northridge
  League of Women Voters collection
Woman's Christian Temperance Union, Southern California Chapter, Los Angeles
  Letters, minutes, and miscellany

GOVERNMENT DOCUMENTS AND REPORTS

Most of the government reports cited were reprinted in the California *Assembly Journal* or *Senate Journal*. For these reports, the specific issues of the *Journal* in which they were printed have been cited. All other government reports without specific references to their location can be found in research libraries throughout the state.

Board of Directors of the California State Prison, Reports, 1855–79.
California. *Assembly Journal*. Reports of special and select committees, 1855–1941.
California. *Senate Journal*. Reports, testimony, and documents, 1851–1933.
California Department of Corrections. *Program Analysis and Recommendations*. Program Planning Report, vol. 2. Sacramento, April 1978.
California Prison Commission. *Annual Report of the California Prison Commission*. San Francisco, 1867–74.
California State Board of Charities and Corrections, Reports, 1904–20.
California State Board of Prison Directors, Reports, 1880–1941.

————. *Rules and Regulations for the Paroling of Prisoners*. Sacramento: State Publications Office, 1909.
California Statutes, 1851–1945.

SECONDARY SOURCES

Beaumont, Gustave de, and Alexis de Tocqueville. *On the Penitentiary System in the United States*. Translated by Francis Lieber. Carbondale: Southern Illinois University Press, 1964.

Berk, Richard A., David Rauma, Sheldon L. Messinger, and Thomas F. Cooley. "A Test of the Stability of Punishment Hypothesis: The Case of California, 1851–1970." *American Sociological Review*, 46 (December 1981): 805–29.

Black, Jack. *The Big Break at Folsom: A Story of the Revolt of Prison Tyranny*. San Francisco: San Francisco Bulletin, c. 1908.

Brown, Michael D. *History of Folsom Prison*. Represa, Calif.: Folsom Prison, 1978.

Burke, Robert E. *Olson's New Deal for California*. Berkeley: University of California Press, 1953.

Carleton, Mark T. *Politics and Punishment: The History of the Louisiana State Penal System*. Baton Rouge: Louisiana State University Press, 1971.

Carter, Anne Louise. "History and Treatment of Women in the Penal Institutions of California." Master's thesis, University of California, Berkeley, 1949.

Chernin, Milton. "A History of California State Administration in the Field of Penology." Master's thesis, University of California, Los Angeles, 1929.

Conley, John A. "Prisons, Production, and Profit: Reconsidering the Importance of Prison Industries." *Journal of Social History* 14, no. 2 (1980): 257–75.

————. "Revising Conceptions About the Origin of Prisons: The Importance of Economic Considerations." *Social Science Quarterly* 62 (June 1981): 247–58.

Duffy, Clinton T., as told to Dean Jennings. *The San Quentin Story*. New York: Greenwood Press, 1968.

Eriksson, Torsten. *The Reformers: An Historical Survey of Pioneer Experiments in the Treatment of Criminals*. New York: Elsevier, 1976.

Ford, Tirey L. *California State Prisons: Their History, Development, and Management*. San Francisco: Star Press, 1910.

Foucault, Michel. *Discipline and Punish: The Birth of the Prison*. London: Allen Lane, 1977.

Freedman, Estelle B. *Their Sisters' Keepers: Women's Prison Reform in America, 1830–1930*. Ann Arbor: University of Michigan Press, 1981.

Friedman, Lawrence M. "Plea Bargaining in Historical Perspective." *Law & Society Review*, 13, no. 2 (1979): 247–59.

Friedman, Lawrence M., and Robert B. Percival. *The Roots of Justice: Crime and Punishment in Alameda County, California, 1870–1910*. Chapel Hill: University of North Carolina Press, 1981.

Garbutt, Mary Alderman. *Victories of Four Decades: A History of the Women's Christian Temperance Union of Southern California, 1833–1924.* Los Angeles: WCTU, 1924.

Gill, Howard B. "Correctional Philosophy and Architecture." *Journal of Criminal Law, Criminology, and Police Science* 53, no. 3 (1962): 312–22.

Griffith, Griffith J. "The Autobiography of Griffith Jenkins Griffith." Typescript, Special Collections, University of California, Los Angeles, n. d.

Guinn, J. M. *Some California Place Names, (Their Origin and Meaning).* Tenth Annual Report, 1906. Los Angeles: Historical Society of Southern California, 1906.

Henderson, Charles Richmond, ed. *Penal and Reformatory Institutions.* New York: Charities Publication Committee, 1910. Reprint. Dubuque, Iowa: Brown Reprints, n.d.

———. *Prison Reform: Correction and Prevention.* New York: Charities Publication Committee, 1910. Reprint. Dubuque, Iowa: Brown Reprints, n.d.

Highton, E. R. *Observations on the Qualifications and Professional Training of Officers for Prisons and Reformatories.* San Francisco: California Prison Commission, 1882.

Hindus, Michael Stephen. *Prison and Plantation: Crime, Justice, and Authority in Massachusetts and South Carolina, 1767–1878.* Chapel Hill: University of North Carolina Press, 1980.

Johnston, Norman. *The Human Cage: A Brief History of Prison Architecture.* New York: Walker & Co., 1973.

Kirker, Harold. *California's Architectural Frontier: Style and Tradition in the Nineteenth Century.* San Marino: Huntington Library, 1960.

Lamott, Kenneth. *Chronicles of San Quentin: The Biography of a Prison.* New York: David McKay Co., 1961.

Lewis, Orlando F. *The Development of American Prisons and Prison Customs, 1776–1845, with Special Reference to Early Institutions in the State of New York.* Albany: Prison Association of New York, 1922.

McKelvey, Blake. *American Prisons: A History of Good Intentions.* Montclair, N.J.: Patterson Smith, 1977.

Melossi, Dario, and Massimo Pavarini. *The Prison and the Factory: Origins of the Penitentiary System.* Translated by Glynis Cousin. London: Macmillan, 1981.

Messinger, Sheldon L., John E. Berecochea, David Rauma, and Richard A. Berk. "The Foundations of Parole in California." *Law & Society Review,* 19, no. 1 (1985): 69–106.

Miller, Eleanor. *When Memory Calls.* Gardena, Calif.: Institute Press, 1936.

Moore, J. Wess. *Glimpse of Prison Life.* Gardena, Calif.: Institute Press, c. 1910.

Morales, Richard. "History of the California Institution for Women, 1927–1960: A Woman's Regime." Ph.D. diss. University of California, Riverside, 1980.

Olson, Gordon L. "I Felt Like I Must Be Entering . . . Another World." *Annals of Wyoming* 47, no. 2 (1975): 152–90.

Patterson, James T. *The New Deal and the States: Federalism in Transition.* Princeton: Princeton University Press, 1969.

Pierson, William H., Jr. *American Buildings and Their Architects: The Colonial and Neo-Classical Styles.* Garden City, N.Y.: Anchor Books, 1976.

Prison Reform League. *Crimes and Criminals.* Los Angeles: Prison Reform League, 1910.

Rothman, David J. *Conscience and Convenience: The Asylum and its Alternatives in Progressive America.* Boston: Little, Brown and Co., 1980.

———. *Discovery of the Asylum: Social Order and Disorder in the New Republic.* Boston: Little, Brown and Co. 1971.

Schlesinger, Arthur M., Jr. *The Politics of Upheaval.* Boston: Houghton Mifflin Co., 1960.

Scudder, Kenyon J. *Between Dark and Daylight.* Berkeley: University of California Regional Oral History Office, 1972.

———. *Prisoners Are People.* New York: Doubleday & Sons, 1952.

Sellin, Thorsten. "Corrections in Historical Perspective." Reprinted in *Correctional Institutions*, edited by Robert Carter, Daniel Glazer, and Leslie T. Wilkins. Philadelphia: J. B. Lippincott, 1972.

Stanley, Leo L. *Men At Their Worst.* New York: Appleton-Century, 1940.

Voigt, Lloyd L. *History of California State Correctional Administration from 1930 to 1948.* San Francisco: n.p., 1949.

Wilkins, James H. "The Evolution of a State Prison." *San Francisco Bulletin.* June 13, 1918 through July 1, 1918.

Wines, Enoch Cobb, and Theodore Dwight. *Report on the Prisons and Reformatories of the United States and Canada, Made to the Legislature of New York, January, 1867.* 1867. Reprint. Montclair, N.J.: Patterson Smith, 1976.

Other titles in the series Law in the American West include:

Volume 1
Christian G. Fritz
Federal Justice in California: The Court of Ogden Hoffman, 1851–1891

Volume 2
Gordon Morris Bakken
Practicing Law in Frontier California